Amazon FBA And Dropshipping Bible

Your 3-Days

Beginner To Expert Guide In

Building A Passive Income Empire

Using Amazon FBA Or Dropshipping

Online Business

By

Michael Ezeanaka

www.MichaelEzeanaka.com

Disclaimer

This publication is designed to provide competent and reliable information regarding the subject matter covered. However, it is sold with the understanding that the author is not engaged in rendering investment or other professional advice. Laws and practices often vary from state to state and country to country and if investment or other expert assistance is required, the services of a professional should be sought. The author specifically disclaims any liability that is incurred from the use or application of the contents of this book.

Table of Contents

BOOK I – AMAZON FBA

BOOK 2 - DROPSHIPPING

Introduction

Today, millions of people all over the world do their shopping online. And one great thing that came out of this whole internet shopping phenomenon is the opportunity given to individual sellers to compete on equal footing against big companies and retailers. Setting up an e-commerce business is not as costly as opening a physical store that requires you to pay for monthly rent, utilities, and so on. You can set up shop in your basement and run your business behind the computer in the comforts of your home.

One of the most popular e-commerce websites and online retailers is Amazon. In fact, according to one study, Amazon is the starting point of 44% of online shoppers, with Google trailing behind at 33%. Moreover, 40% of people who live in the United States buy at least one item every month from the website. No wonder it has become the central hub of online buying and selling.

And if you are specifically thinking of selling your own stuff with your own private label on Amazon, and have them take care of storage and fulfillment to customers, you have come to the right place because this book will teach you everything you need to know about Amazon FBA, which is exactly what you need. Combine your hard work and business acumen with high quality products and Amazon FBA, and you will surely be well on your way to great success.

Without further ado, let's get right into it!

Chapter 1

Amazon FBA Business Model Explained

Before you get too excited and start sending all your products to Amazon, you should first understand what the Amazon FBA business model is all about. Amazon FBA literally stands for Fulfilled by Amazon and it gives third-party vendors access to Amazon's facilities and services. Launched in 2016, Amazon FBA is just one of the different business models that Amazon offers to its partner sellers. If you register to this program, you are taking advantage of Amazon's huge facilities, efficient cataloguing, advanced shipping, and customer service. How cool is that?
Amazon gets half of its sales from third party vendors like you, and 66% of the top 10,000 Amazon vendors use FBA.

How The Business Model Works

You send all your products, whether used or brand new, to one of Amazon's fulfillment centers. These are huge warehouses where they store all the products sent by sellers like you. These fulfillment centers are massive, the largest covers an area of 1,264,200 square feet and is located in Texas. The warehouses are run not only by employees but also by robots. As of 2018, they have 75 fulfillment centers across North America. Add to this the additional 25 sortation centers, where items are sorted to be delivered to different locations, and you get an idea how Amazon can handle such a huge undertaking.

When your products reach one of these fulfillment centers, they will then be sorted and catalogued. You do not have to worry about your products getting lost or damaged in these huge warehouses because they are well taken care of by employees and robots, and everything is computerized. And on the off-chance (which means it is an extremely rare occurrence) that one of your products gets damaged while in the fulfillment centers, you can consider it sold because Amazon will pay for the full retail price of the item.

Now you just wait for someone to buy your item listed on the Amazon website. Amazon will handle the whole transaction when a customer buys your listed product on the website. The whole process is automated, which makes it a lot faster.

Since the items in the warehouse are assigned their unique inventory code, it is easier to find them among the hundreds of shelves lined up inside the huge warehouse. The item will be packaged and delivered to the buyer by Amazon on your behalf.

Once the item is delivered to the customer, Amazon will follow up to ensure that there are no problems with the shipment and that the customer is satisfied with the order. Amazon also handles customer service for FBA items, and also returns and refunds, with your assistance of course.

So what are your responsibilities as a seller? You still have something to do, right? Of course, you do. Amazon FBA just shoulders half of the work so that you can focus your attention and efforts on other things that are also important when managing an e-commerce business.

As an FBA seller, you still have to:

1. Determine the products that you want to sell.

Amazon will not help you choose what products you want to sell, and they also will not source your products for you. You still have to do your research on what products sell well, and where you can source them. You also have to know how much the products are going for online and in physical stores so that you can have a rough estimate on how much profit you will be getting. One important tip to remember is to sell fast-moving items because you have to pay for their storage in the fulfillment center.

2. Monitor your inventory levels.

It is your responsibility as a seller to check if you still have enough products to sell that are in storage. Since these items are in the fulfillment centers, it is easy to lose track of how much you still have because you cannot see them in person, unlike when you keep your stocks in your own place. Although Amazon will let you know if your inventory is running low, it is still up to you to be proactive and ensure that you have enough products to sell.

3. Market and promote your products.

This does not mean you have to pay expensive TV or print ads. Maybe that's how it was many years ago. Online advertising is different. It is a lot less expensive and you need to use the right techniques more than money. If you are a re-seller of brand name products that are already highly-ranked, you may no longer need to do this step because the big corporations already have their own million-dollar ads and billboards. But if you are selling your own custom products or private label products, then you have to do this step and make sure that people can see your products. Remember that Amazon has millions of products listed online, which makes marketing an essential step if you want people to find your items for sale.

What are the benefits of Amazon FBA?

Based on what you have read so far, you probably get an idea about the kinds of benefits that you will get if you decide to sell your own private label products using Amazon FBA. But to give you a clearer view of the different benefits of Amazon FBA that can help you decide if it is something that you want to try, continue reading the next points.

1. Efficient logistics, cheaper shipping rates, and faster delivery time

If you are selling a few products, it is easier to handle everything on your own and in your own house. You do not really need to rent a place for storage or to hire people. But if you are thinking of starting an e-commerce business as a main source of income, and you are going to sell a lot of products, then you need a more efficient way to handle and ship all your items on time. And hiring professionals to do all these things for you may be expensive. With Amazon, you are taking advantage of their expertise and experience with shipping and logistics. After all, they are the biggest e-commerce website in the world right now, and being efficient goes with the territory.

Moreover, when shipping items, you have to consider different rules and regulations. Different factors affect shipping fees such as the weight and size of the product, the kind of product you are going to ship, and so on. You also need to research about international shipping (in case you decide to make your products available to international buyers), areas served by the courier, prohibited and restricted commodities, insurance, and so many things. If you use Amazon FBA, you do not have to worry because Amazon will take care of these things for you.

Third party sellers like yourself and online shoppers both benefit from this because the entire shipping process is a lot faster. After all, your items are already in their warehouses and they have partnerships with big courier companies because they ship thousands, if not millions, of items worldwide. Amazon also has fulfillment centers all over the world, which allows them to deliver customer orders within just a couple of days. This is because when a customer buys a product from you, they do not necessarily get the exact item that you sent to Amazon. Amazon sort like products together, so if a customer buys a specific item, say, a Mickey Mouse t-shirt, and you live in the United States and your buyer lives in Canada, they will search for a similar item in the fulfillment center closest to the buyer, which significantly shortens the delivery period and also makes shipping fee a lot cheaper.

Shipping is also generally cheaper if you let Amazon handle it for you because, as I mentioned previously, they have partnerships with big shipping companies and they can get discounts because they ship a lot of items (i.e. economy of scale). And to attract higher sales, Amazon passes on this incentive to the sellers and buyers. You, as a seller, can get reduced shipping costs when sending your products to one of their fulfillment centers. And FBA products are often eligible for free shipping, especially to buyers who are Amazon Prime members. It boosts Amazon's sales, attracts more buyers for you, and saves customers on shipping costs. It is a win-win-win type of situation for all parties involved.

2. More free time for you

Managing an e-commerce business can be time-consuming especially if you handle everything by yourself — from sourcing products to sell, taking pictures, storing, packaging, pricing, shipping, and handling customer service. If you leverage the Amazon FBA business model, you are freeing up a lot of your time that you can use to concentrate on more important things such as choosing products for your online store, sourcing the products, and taking great photos. And the more time you spend on these things, the higher quality of products and the better photos you will have in your online store. And besides, these are the fun parts of selling products online.

Shopping for things to resell or making them yourself is what makes people do online selling. A lot of sellers also enjoy photography so taking pictures of their products is just like a hobby for most of them. The boring parts of managing an e-commerce business are the shipping and logistics, and also handling returns and customer complaints. And thankfully, this can all be taken care of by Amazon through FBA.

You can use your free time to research on what products to sell, how to improve your products, how to promote your products, the current prices of similar products on the market, and how to scale up your business. You can also focus on taking great pictures of your items for sale. Remember that in online selling, pictures paint a thousand words, and it is sometimes what makes or breaks a sale. If your picture does not look good, some people will question the quality of your product and will not buy them, no matter how great your product actually is.

Aside from spending your free time doing things to grow your business, you can also use it for doing personal stuff, such as travelling, spending time with your loved ones, learning a new hobby, and so on. It gives you the perfect balance between your business and your personal life. Some people even continue working their regular full-time job while managing their e-commerce business.

3. Huge storage space

You can live in a tiny house and still sell huge products without the need for a large storage space if you are using Amazon FBA because all of your stuff will be stored in their humongous fulfillment centers. Not having enough storage space at home sometimes stops a lot of people from selling big items or keeping a large inventory. Your house or even a rented commercial space can only hold a limited amount of stuff.

You do not have to worry about boxes and packages cluttered in your living room or bedroom because Amazon takes care of all this. Having boxes and packages that you need to step over inside your house can be hazardous and can cause accidents. You do not want this to happen at all. And renting your own warehouse can be costly, especially if you are just starting because apart from the monthly rent, you have to pay for utilities such as electricity, internet connection, and even water in some instances.

Another good thing about sending your stuff to Amazon is that there is no minimum inventory required. Heck, you can even send just one product if you really do not have any storage at all in your house. Amazon also gives an incentive to sellers whose products move fast, meaning they don't stay for a long time in the storage facility. You can get unlimited storage if your items sell like hotcakes, so to speak.

Moreover, Amazon fulfillment centers have the right kind of storage for certain products. For instance, if you are selling leather bags or shoes, you do not want to store them in your basement where the high humidity and temperature can cause damage to your products.

4. Amazon's good reputation

It is not hard to believe that Amazon is the leading online selling platform because it is reliable, and a lot of buyers and sellers trust its business platform. If you use Amazon FBA, you are also benefiting from Amazon's strong reputation. They have already established their brand name and collaborating with them will do your business a lot of good. For people who are just starting to sell online, selling products through Amazon will bring them higher sales than selling their products through their own website.

Although there is nothing wrong with having your own website, it poses a bigger risk for individual sellers than if they bring their business to a well-known selling platform that already has an established reputation, such as Amazon. And it is even better if you use Amazon FBA because buyers would know that a large company is handling certain aspects of your business for you.

As you establish your own brand and reputation, you can maybe then focus solely on selling on your very own website. But for now, Amazon is the easiest way to get higher sales. In fact, even established companies and sellers still use Amazon as an online selling platform because they know that they will get a higher reach since millions of people are now using Amazon.

5. Handles customer service and returns

This is another one of the less attractive features of having your own business—handling customer service and returns. Before buying a product, some customers already have a lot of question. And this is handled by people who work at Amazon. They have customer service centers that provide support 24/7 through phone calls, emails, and chat. If they have more questions or even complaints upon receiving the item, Amazon will also take care of it for you. This is a really great benefit, especially for people who love the whole mechanics of selling online, but not the part where you have to talk to the customer.

In fact, a lot of people prefer online selling over the traditional form of selling where you have to talk to the person face to face because they are not comfortable at this kind of set up. This is why having someone else do this for you is a great help. Moreover, Amazon customer service representatives are trained to handle different concerns and complaints. They can handle even the most irate customers because that's what they are trained to do.

Another thing that they handle for you is returns. Handling returns can be a hassle because you not only have to deal with upset customers but also the logistics and administrative aspect of having the product returned to you and the payment returned to the customer. They also have to do inspection to check if the item is really damaged before shipping it to the customer or not. All of this is handled by Amazon. Of course, there is a corresponding fee but it is worth the small amount that you have to pay for the work and trouble that they take off your plate.

6. Increase your sales

Ultimately, this is the main goal of all this, why you are selling online and why you are partnering with Amazon. You want to make sure that you have high sales even on a website like Amazon, where you will surely have a lot of competitors. All the benefits that you can enjoy using Amazon FBA boil down to this — attracting more buyers and boosting your sales. You may think that you are getting less because you have to pay Amazon different kinds of fees, but the efficiency and expertise allow you to sell more items at a quicker rate, which means higher sales for you in a shorter period of time. Besides, the fees are worth it because you are using their top-of-the-line facilities and expertise in online selling. You are even saving money because you do not have to pay for your own warehouse and hire staff or assistants who will help you with all of these once your business starts to grow.

What are the disadvantages of Amazon FBA?

Just like with all kinds of business models, Amazon FBA also has disadvantages, although it is already an incredible online selling platform. After all, no business model is perfect. You also need to understand the different disadvantages of Amazon FBA before you decide to use it in your e-commerce business.

1. Amazon FBA costs money

Not everything in life is free, and if you expect to get top notch service and expertise, then you should be willing to pay the price. This is also true if you decide to use Amazon FBA. You have to pay for the storage of your products. The longer your products stay in their fulfillment centers, the more you have to pay. This is why it is important to ensure that your products sell quickly. Do not let them stay in Amazon storage for more than six months.

Be prepared to pay sky-high storage fees if your inventory sits for a long time. Because of this, you have to take this into consideration. Will you still make a profit even after all the storage fees that you paid for that particular item? Although you can sell large items, you have to make sure that they will move fast because this can cost you a lot in terms of storage. It is also not ideal to store cheap items where you only get a small profit in Amazon fulfillment centers because you might end up paying more for the storage than the actual product itself.

2. Monitoring inventory can be challenging

Although you can always ask Amazon about your inventory, it is still more difficult to track your inventory if you do not see them in person. It is hard to determine what products you still have, what's been sitting in storage for months, what you need to re-order, when you need to buy more, and so on. If your inventory is in plain sight, you will be able to know right away which ones are selling and which ones are not. This makes it even more challenging during the holiday season, when people buy a lot of their gifts for their loved ones online and orders come in by the thousands.

3. Co-mingling can be tricky

Amazon sorts similar items together in their fulfillment centers for efficiency. For example, Amazon will group all Adidas Stan Smith sneakers from different sellers together. This means that a person who clicked your listing and purchased the item does not necessarily mean that he will be getting the sneakers that you sent, although he will still get his Stan Smiths. You have the option to take advantage of this feature if you want to.

However, this can be scary for some because not all sellers are reliable and trustworthy. Some even send damaged or counterfeit products, and if you are unlucky and the buyer got that damaged or counterfeit item that another seller has sent, then you will be the one getting the negative feedback. Some legitimate sellers were even banned from selling on Amazon because of this, although this is a rare case.

4. Amazon controls about half of your business

When partnering with Amazon via FBA, you are giving up a lot of control over your business. For example, you cannot choose the kind of packaging that you want for your items and you cannot also add a personal touch such a short thank you note or some customized stickers and freebies into the package because Amazon handles all the packaging and shipping. You cannot tell them to use a silvery packaging paper or use eco-friendly packaging. They do things their way, which is of course more efficient but does not have the personal touch that you would want your buyers to experience when they buy items from your online shop.

5. Product prep can be difficult

You need to follow certain guidelines when sending out your inventory to Amazon. It can be time consuming and tedious, especially for beginners but you will soon get the hang of it after doing it several times. For example, there are different rules to follow for sending multiples of the same products in one package, single products, single products with different parts, and so on. You also have to use the right kind of bag for your items. There are also special instructions for sending adult products, e.g. using a shrink wrap or a black, opaque poly bag. There are so many things to consider when prepping, packaging, and labeling your products to be sent out to Amazon that there is a separate chapter only for this topic, which you will see later on.

Private label business model and other ways of selling on Amazon

This book is all about selling private label products through Amazon FBA. There are different ways to sell on Amazon, and one of them is by selling private label items.

1. Private label

As the name implies, private label means you choose a specific product to sell under your own private label or brand via Amazon FBA. If you are a private label seller, you decide on which product you want to sell, for instance clothes. You source them from a supplier, usually from China, and make them your own private label or brand. A third-party supplier under a contract manufactures the items.

To find products that you can sell under your own private label, you need to do a lot of research and studying, especially involving the market and what sells profitably and what doesn't. You are also responsible for contacting the suppliers or manufacturers. This is something that you cannot delegate to Amazon. You even have the option to have all the products shipped directly to Amazon by the third-party supplier, which means that all you need to do is to sit behind your laptop and manage your whole business.

With private label, you are not hindered by not having enough resources or skills to create the product that you want to sell because you can find a supplier who will do all of these for you. For example, if you want to sell clothes under your own logo or label, you do not really need to be a seamstress or buy all the materials needed for making clothes because all you need to do is to find someone who can do this for you. You can order them in bulk and have the products shipped to Amazon either directly by the manufacturer or by you.

2. Retail arbitrage

This is another way to sell products on Amazon. You search for low-priced branded products online or in retail stores, and resell them on Amazon at a marked up price. Retail arbitrage sellers often go to the clearance racks of giant retail corporations such as Target, Walmart, and Home Depot for their inventory.

For example, there is a sale on school supplies in Target and you are able to purchase a pack of 12 ballpoint pens for a discounted price of $3. You buy them and resell them on Amazon for $8, which is a little lower than their regular price of $12. You still earn a profit even if you sell it at a significantly lower price compared to the regular price. You also have the choice to sell it at the regular price of $12 if you want, especially if you know that these pens are highly sought after.

Private label sellers, on the other hand, only source their products from one manufacturer. The products are also sold under their own brand name while retail arbitrage sellers keep the brand name of their products, unless they want to be sued for intellectual property theft. Retail arbitrage is what a lot of people do when they sell online, especially those who are just part-time sellers who do not have a huge budget to buy things in bulk and establish their own brand name.

3. Wholesale

Buying wholesale from manufacturers and selling them as is on Amazon at a higher price is another way of selling on Amazon. You cannot sell the products under your own name or add value to the products because you are selling products under an established brand name. For example, you can buy wholesale Sony mobile phone cases directly from Sony and sell them as Sony mobile phone cases. You cannot rename the brand and change it to your own private label or you will be sued.

It is a bit similar to private label because you buy in bulk. The main difference is that you go to a manufacturer with the intention of buying their products in bulk and reselling these products while keeping the manufacturer's own brand. With private label selling, you go to a manufacturer and you agree upon a contract that includes buying their products in bulk that suits your business requirements, adding value to these products, and selling them under your own brand.

Wholesale buying and reselling is also kind of similar to retail arbitrage because manufacturers get to keep their own brand name. The main difference is that in wholesale, you source bulk products from one manufacturer, and in retail arbitrage, you source them from many different retailers.

4. Used book sales

Selling used books via Amazon is one of the easiest ways to start an online business that does not require a lot of capital. Financial risk is much lower when you sell used books. After all, you can just sell whatever you already have at home and you can easily buy used books for just a few dollars. Moreover, selling used books will also not get you as much complaints or returns from consumers as compared to selling other types of products unless you mistakenly sent the wrong book. You can even use the money that you earn from selling used books to launch your own private label business.

Pros and cons of private label vs. other ways of selling on Amazon

Private label vs. retail arbitrage

The drawback of retail arbitrage is that you have to continuously search for items on sale at different places. With private label, you already have a contract with one supplier, unless you decide to change your supplier or add more products to sell, which makes sourcing a lot easier. Your shop will also have more variety in terms of type or brand if you do retail arbitrage whereas private label selling means fewer types of products and only one brand (your private brand) to sell. The amount of products you can buy depends solely on your budget if you decide to do private label selling. On the other hand, the amount of products you can sell using retail arbitrage depends not only on your budget but also on the availability of the product. The pens that you were able to buy for $3 and resell for $8 may no longer be available next time there is another sale. Because of this unpredictability, it is difficult to get consistent sales with retail arbitrage. Your profit margins will be variable, depending on how much you were able to get the item for.

Going back to our pen example, you might be able to find them again the next time they are on sale, but the discounted price may not be the same. It may be higher ($5 for 12 pens) or lower ($1 for all 12!). Retail arbitrage depends a lot on chance (of stumbling upon great deals) while private label is all about careful planning. This is why selling private labeled products has a bigger potential to grow, but at the same time, the risks of losing a lot of money is also much higher, especially if you are selling a single type of product in your shop.

Private label vs. wholesale

Both methods of selling get their products in bulk from one supplier, which means that sourcing is easy for both. And since both buy products in bulk, profit margins can easily be determined because they already have an idea about the base price of the products, and how much they go for in the market.

The main difference between the two, as mentioned earlier, is the branding. When you buy wholesale from a manufacturer, you resell the products under the manufacturer's brand. When you do private label selling, you can add value to your product and sell them under your own brand. Private label selling gives you more control because you can do whatever you want with the products once you buy them from the manufacturer.

Another difference between wholesale and private label is that in wholesale, you have to find a manufacturer that is not already selling directly on Amazon. You see that a lot of these popular brands also have their own accounts on Amazon. And how can you compete with the manufacturer selling their products on the same online selling platform?

But if you really become successful in private label selling, you can turn your online business into a multimillion company. Your name will be associated with your brand, which you created all on your own. Multimillionaires did not become rich by reselling products that they buy from existing brands. They created their own brands, and source the products somewhere else. Or better yet, you can create your own product. But that is another topic for another day.

Private label vs. retail arbitrage and wholesale

Basically, you are building your own brand from scratch with private label selling, unlike wholesale and retail arbitrage. It involves a higher financial risk than the other two but the rewards are also much greater if your business becomes successful. With retail arbitrage and wholesale reselling, the products that you sell already have an established brand. You do not really need to launch or promote them because the manufacturers already have their own ads for their products on different media such as TV, radio, print, and online. All you need to do is to make sure that your shop is visible enough so that when the customers search for the products, they will see your online store on top. People already know the products and the brand that you are selling. With private selling, you have to do a launch to let people know about your brand and the kind of products that you sell. You also have to make sure that you promote your products by advertising and making your shop more visible online.

Who are the stakeholders in the private label business model?

The three main stakeholders in this kind of business model are the following: the business owner (you), the manufacturer, and Amazon. In between and under these categories, there are minor players that make up the whole business model and make things run more smoothly and efficiently. Let's discuss the major stakeholders first.

1. The business owner

This refers to you, the person who has the idea to start an online business selling niche products under his own brand. You are responsible for determining the kind of products that you can sell through Amazon or even other channels. This means that you have to spend time doing research. There are already thousands of sellers of clothes. You can still sell clothes, but you need to find a niche where no one or very few has gone before. For example, you can sell funny hats instead of normal looking hats.

Your products need to stand out from the rest if you want people to notice and buy them. As the business owner, you are also responsible for finding the right manufacturer that can provide you with your orders in bulk. Again, research is your most powerful tool. It is also necessary that you have enough funds to make a bulk order from the manufacturer, pay Amazon fees, and cover miscellaneous expenses.

Setting up an Amazon account and registering for their Amazon FBA service is also your sole responsibility. Creating your own brand (e.g. coming up with your brand name and logo), prepping the products, adding your listings, monitoring your inventory, tracking your shipment, filing your tax, and so on are just some additional responsibilities of the seller. You can also choose your own freight forwarder to have the products shipped out to Amazon.

2. The manufacturer

Once you have found the manufacturer that meets all your business requirements, you can now contact them and start doing business with them under a contract that both of you agreed upon. Your chosen supplier is responsible for manufacturing the items that you ordered—whether it is 1,000 units of funny hats or 500 pieces of planners. If you have your own design that you want to sell, you can contact a manufacturer who can make the products for you according to your own specifications. If you just have an idea but you have not created a design of your own, you can simply find a manufacturer through different channels such as Alibaba, which is basically like China's Amazon.

You pay for the finished products, which means that the manufacturer is responsible for finding the materials required for making the products and paying for the workers who are going to make the products. All of these are accounted for when they quote you a price. Once the products are finished, the manufacturer has to find a shipping company to have your orders delivered either to you or directly to Amazon. It's all up to you.

3. Amazon

The third key player in this whole business model is, of course, Amazon. Whether you decide to sell via FBA or FBM (stands for fulfilled by merchant, meaning you just use Amazon as an online selling platform but you take care of the fulfillment aspect), you still need to use Amazon's services. Amazon's involvement begins when you decide to sell your products through their website. After registering, you need to send your items to their fulfillment centers. You can choose to ship using Amazon's partner shippers. With the FBA business model, Amazon has added responsibilities, such as storage of your goods, sorting, shipping to customers, and handling customer complaints and returns.

4. Shippers

The shippers are responsible for moving the products from the manufacturer to you as the seller or to Amazon's fulfillment center. They are also responsible for shipping the orders to the customer, and reverse shipping in case the customer wants to return or exchange the product. Basically, shipping the products to one of Amazon's fulfillment centers can be done by the manufacturer or by the seller. It can be a little tricky if your manufacturer is located overseas, like in China, because shipping can be more expensive, especially if you decide to do air freight.

The better option for international shipping is sea freight, especially if the items are big and heavy. It is cheaper but it takes much longer for the items to reach their destination. If you have the products with you, you also have the option to use traditional courier services such as FedEx or UPS via Amazon Partnered Carrier Program.

And when a customer buys the product, Amazon will deliver the order using their partner courier, mainly UPS, or FedEx and DHL in places that are not serviced by UPS.

5. Inspectors and prep services

Prepping your products to be shipped to Amazon can be challenging because Amazon has strict requirements. To make your life easier, you can simply hire inspectors and prep companies to do these things for you. These companies are responsible for inspecting the items to ensure that they are not damaged or counterfeit and that they adhere to Amazon's strict standards, packing of products, labeling, sorting, photography of products, and forwarding of shipment to Amazon fulfillment centers.

This is especially useful if you are buying from a manufacturer which is located overseas or far from where you live. The prepping company and inspector will ensure that the goods are in good condition and they are packaged, labeled, and sorted according to Amazon's requirements. This saves you a lot of time and trouble because goods that do not pass the standards of Amazon's warehouses will be sent back to the manufacturer or the seller, depending on where it came from. Some examples of these companies are FBAinspection, FBAshipuk, and McKenzie services, to name a few. These companies ensure that your products are perfect before they are shipped to Amazon. You have the option not to hire the services of inspectors and prep companies but if you want to make sure that the whole process will go smoothly, it is best to work with these professionals. This is especially helpful for sellers who have to prepare a high volume of orders. As a seller, it is your responsibility to communicate with the manufacturer and prepping companies the schedule and timings of pickup or delivery.

6. Others

Aside from these, you might also want to hire someone who will create your brand logo. This is an important step that a lot of private label sellers take for granted, thinking they can just use any logo that they come up with. Your brand is important, and it is best to hire a professional graphic designer who can make your brand logo. If you have the talent to do these kinds of things, then go ahead and make your own logo. If not, and all you can do is create random shapes in Paint, then the best thing for you to do is hire a professional. You can hire plenty of good professionals from Fiverr or Upwork. Searching the keyword *"Logo Design"* on Fiverr will bring up a list of freelancers, go through their portfolio and reviews and choose one that meets your taste and budget.

Once your company grows, you should also consider hiring a professional number cruncher a.k.a. an accountant. He will be responsible for balancing your business' books to check how much you are earning, and if you are earning in the first place. This is a must, especially if you are shelling out thousands of dollars to start this business. You also do not want to get in trouble by filing the wrong tax forms and returns. All of these can be done by your accountant.

Pretty soon, as your company continues to grow, you should also think about hiring your own lawyer, who can look over your contracts with manufacturers and suppliers, and also who can give you legal advice in case somebody decided to sue you for something. You might also need to hire your own staff or assistance who can do menial tasks for you so that you can focus on more important things. All of these are a must once your business becomes huge and you start earning hundreds of thousands of dollars.

Chapter 2

Getting Started

Now that you have an idea about how Amazon FBA works, you should now learn the step-by-step procedure for getting started on your e-commerce business. It is not as difficult as you think. Maybe as you are starting, you find it a bit challenging with all the people, tools, and processes involved. But as you progress, the entire process will become second nature to you. And the more you feel comfortable doing it, the more efficient your business will be.

Steps on how to start private label selling via Amazon FBA

This is assuming that you already have the money to start a business, because it's easier to progress when you have the financial wherewithal. If you haven't got the money, don't worry. The last chapter of the book, **Credit Card And Credit Repair Secrets** goes into detail with regards to different sources of funds you can explore for your business.

Later on, you will get a lot of information regarding the costs and fees involved in starting an Amazon FBA private label business. For now, here are the things that you need to do to get started. Although each of these will be discussed in length and depth in the next few chapters, you still need to have a clear idea of the step-by-step procedure that you need to do to start a private label business via Amazon FBA.

1. Determine the product that you want to sell

This requires a lot of brainstorming and research on your end. You cannot just simply start selling a product because that's what you like - although selling something that you like is also important because it adds passion to what you do. You should be selling products that the market demands for. Otherwise, no one will buy your goods.

You can research about the types of products that are selling online. Your first stop should be Amazon itself. Check the different categories and look for interesting products. There is one category called "Hot New Releases" and you might just be able to get ideas from here. You can also simply Google the top-selling products on Amazon. You can also look for unique products in different social media platforms. Check the pages of popular influencers and find out what they are currently using or wearing.

Sometimes, inspiration will strike when you are not looking for it, maybe when you are window-shopping in your favorite boutique or even when you are having a conversation with your friend. You will know and feel when your idea is worth pursuing because you will feel excited to start your business.

2. Look for a manufacturer or supplier

Now that you already have an idea about the kind of product that you want to sell, you should now start searching for a supplier who can manufacture the products for you. If you can find a manufacturer or a supplier in your area, lucky you because you can easily visit the company in person and check the products that they make. You can also talk to them in person, which makes it easier to communicate your needs. If not, you can always check overseas suppliers.

A lot of Amazon private label sellers get their products from manufacturers located in China. How do they find these Chinese suppliers? Through Alibaba, AliExpress etc. Alibaba is like the yellow pages of Chinese manufacturers. You can contact the manufacturer through the app. You will see the retail price per unit and the minimum number of orders that they accept. You can also ask for a sample if you want to see if the quality of their products is up to your standards. It is best to contact more than one supplier, maybe 3 to 5, just to give you more options and to get the best deal.

3. Finalize your brand

While you are waiting for your products, you can use your time creating your brand. That is, if you have not created it before you started searching for the product. You might already have a vague idea of what you want your brand to look like but you still need to finalize everything. Since you are selling private label products, you can put your brand name or logo on the packaging or on the product itself. In some cases, it is best to already have a finalized brand name and logo so that the manufacturer can already add it to your product, for example, if you are planning to sell clothes. If not, you can always use other ways to incorporate your brand to the product.

You can maybe add a sticker or a tag that carries your brand name and logo. You can also design your own packaging, although it will still be hidden inside the poly bags that Amazon requires you to use and the final layer of packaging for when the item is going to be shipped to the customer. You should try to include your shop's contact details on the packaging or tag, such as website URL, phone numbers, social media pages, and other useful information that will lead the customer to your shop.

4. Create your Amazon account

This may be complicated for some people, but you have to master the Amazon website because this will be your selling platform. All you need to do is to go to the website and sign up if you do not have an Amazon seller account yet. If you do, you still need to create your Amazon FBA account by simply going to the Amazon FBA home page. The step-by-step procedure for creating your Amazon FBA account will be discussed later on in this chapter.

5. List your items

After creating your Amazon seller account, you can now start adding your listings. You can do this even when the products haven't arrived yet as long as you already have the photos and the specifications of the products. Be sure to tick the box that says you want Amazon to ship your products and to provide customer service to take advantage of Amazon FBA.

6. Prepare your inventory

Once the manufacturer is done with your orders, you can now start preparing your inventory to be shipped to Amazon's fulfillment center. You can hire a prepping company to do this for you, as discussed previously. Or you can do it yourself if you think you can follow Amazon's policies regarding product prepping.

7. Ship your items

Your products are now ready to be shipped to Amazon. Once your products arrive at Amazon's fulfillment centers, your listing will become active.

Once your products reach Amazon's warehouse, the rest of the process is pretty much Amazon's responsibility. You can sit back and wait for the orders to come in, but it is also important to keep promoting and advertising your business so that your products and brand will become more visible.

How to create an Amazon seller central account

This is what will connect you to Amazon. You cannot do business with them without an account, especially if you are planning to sell via FBA. Assuming that you don't have an account with Amazon yet, here are the steps that you need to follow.

1. Go to Amazon website

Just go to this website URL and click the Start selling button. Since you do not have an account yet, just click the Create your Amazon account button and enter the following details: your name, your email address (it is better to use a business email address, which is different from your personal email), and password (should be at least 6 characters).

2. Professional vs. individual

You need to choose what type of account you want to have as a seller—professional or individual. You might say, of course the obvious choice is professional because this is your business. However, it is important to note the differences between the two so that you can choose which plan will work best for you.

For both plants, you will have the option to sell via FBA. The main difference between the two is the number of items that you can sell per month. If you are going to sell more than 40 items per month, then it is best to choose the professional account. If your inventory will only have less than 40 items per month, then choose individual account. A professional seller plan also has a monthly fee of $39.99 per month while an individual seller plan doesn't require you to pay an upfront fee. However, individual sellers are required to pay $0.99 every time they sell an item. This fee is waived for professional sellers. If you are confident that your items will sell like hotcakes, then go ahead and pay for the professional seller plan.

If you are not yet sure, you can always try the individual seller plan first, then later on upgrade to professional plan as you start getting the hang of selling on Amazon.

3. Seller information

The details that you need to provide after creating a username and password are your legal name (for taxation purposes), the name of your business (or your display name) and the website URL (if you are already selling online), and your contact number (mobile or telephone). You can choose whether you want to receive a phone call or an SMS for your PIN verification. Read the seller agreement and tick the box. If you are an international seller, meaning you don't reside in the US, you need to read additional important information, which is also on the same page.

When asked to provide your business display name, it is best to use your brand name because this is the one that buyers will see next to your items. It should represent the kind of products that you sell and it should also be easy to remember.

Click next.

4. Verification

You will receive a phone call or a text message to verify your phone number and your account.

5. Set up your billing method

You also need to provide your credit card details for billing and bank account details for deposits. Just give your bank account number and routing number that you can find in the package given to you when you first opened your bank account or if you already lost it, you can just contact your bank. You will also see here your selling plan (professional vs. individual) and the corresponding fees that you need to pay. This is also the part where you can choose Amazon FBA as a way of selling.

6. Provide your tax information

This is a mandatory step and basically, it is just like filling out your W-9 form. You will be asked different questions about your tax information such as the income beneficiary, if you are a U.S. citizen, your name as shown on your income tax return, and your federal tax classification. This will be validated by Amazon.

7. Product information

This is an optional step for account setup. You can do this later if you are pressed for time. The questions that you will be asked are if you have Universal Product Codes (UPC) for your items, if you manufacture and brand your products, and the number of different products that you want to sell.

Voila! Your Amazon seller account is now set up! The next step is exploring your seller central space, which is all about managing your inventory and orders. This is where you will add your listings. It has several tabs that include Inventory, Pricing, Orders, Advertising, Reports, and Performance.

What tools are required?

When it comes to selling online, you will have a lot of options with regards to different tools that you can use to help you boost your brand and sales. These tools also help you run your business more smoothly and efficiently. Some of the tools that you should know as an Amazon FBA seller are as follows:

For niche research

If you have a product in mind and you want to know if it has a good market, you can use certain software for niche research such as Viral Launch. It'll help you find the best ideas with regards to what products to sell, sales estimates for these products, competitor tracking, opportunity scores (products that are considered good opportunities will be given a high score), and many more. You cannot simply rely on your gut instinct when it comes to choosing the best products to sell, especially if a lot of money is involved.

For keyword research

In the world of online selling, keyword is KING. You may have the best products, but if you are not using the right keywords for them, people will still not see them. You need to familiarize yourself with SEO and how it works in online selling. Viral Launch also provides keyword research assistance. You can also try Merchant Words, Keyword Tool and Sonar-tool.

For URL shortener

You do not want to scare your customers away by giving them links that are too long, and include so many weird looking characters. You should shorten your URLs using software such as Bitly and Google Short URL.

For calculating profit margins, fees, etc.

There is a tool called FBA Calculator for Amazon (you can't get any more specific than that!) that helps you calculate your profit margins. Calculating your profit margins while selling via Amazon FBA is not as simple as calculating typical profit margins because there is a lot of fees involved. There is also a specific calculator for freight rate called Amazon FBA Freight Rate Calculator.

For managing feedbacks and reviews

This type of software helps boost your rating as a seller because it helps you send feedback request emails to customers. Sometimes, customers do not make an effort to write a review when they purchase a product because no one is urging them to do it. When they receive an email from you asking them to write a review, they will remember and will be more than willing to do it because you made a specific request. One example of this type of software is AMZFinder. It gives you 500 free auto-emails per month that will help you receive more positive reviews, which can in turn boost your sales and improve your ranking.

For managing reimbursements

Amazon may be a huge company that has topnotch facilities and efficient staff but just like all companies, they still make mistakes. Sometimes, these mistakes can cost sellers money. Maybe they mishandled a product and when the customer received it, it's already damaged. Or maybe they unknowingly received a counterfeit item from another seller, and they sent out this particular item to your buyer, and when the buyer received the item, he understandably returned the item and asked for a refund. Things like these can happen, and it is a normal part of running a business. But you can minimize your losses using software such as AMZ Refund and Refunds Manager that help manage eligible reimbursements.

For multi-channel selling and inventory management

If you are selling on other platforms and websites, or if you have a high volume of inventory, you should consider using a tool that will help you manage all your listings. They will let you know when you are running low on supplies so that you can restock. They can also help integrate multiple online selling platforms into one system to make it easier for you to track your sales, orders, and inventory. Some examples of these software are Brightpearl, RestockPro, and Forecastly.

For product content optimization

Sometimes, duplicate content makes it difficult for search engines to choose which version is more relevant. Search engines also penalize duplicate contents, which is why some pages do not get high rankings even though they have similar content to those that are on the first few pages. Maybe you have been penalized by Google, and you just don't know it. Certain tools can help you with these kinds of issues such as Content26, Geek Speak Commerce, and mobiReady.

For pricing solutions

In such a huge market platform like Amazon, you will surely have several competitors, no matter how unique your niche may be. And if there are multiple sellers selling the same product, where will the buyer take his business? To the seller which offers the lowest price. This is also what you will do if you are the buyer. This is why it is important to monitor and compare prices of the kinds of products that you sell. You can use certain tools designed for this such as Price Checker 2.0, Appeagle, and Feedvisor.

For product launch

You need to launch your product, especially since you are a private label seller. The main goal of doing a product launch is to let people know about your products and also about your brand. Certain tools can help you with this such as <u>Viral Launch</u>, SnagShout, and iLoveToReview.

For accessing online courses, mentors, and community of sellers

Beginners like you will benefit a lot if you have someone who can give you advice regarding selling on Amazon. If you have extra money, you can hire a mentor in consulting marketplaces such as Clarity, where you have to pay per amount of time spent with the mentor. For an online course, you can try Proven Amazon Course, which includes Proven Private Label. You can also search for online communities of Amazon sellers. Some forums that you should check out are Ecommerce Fuel, Amazon Seller Central, and Reddit's Fulfillment by Amazon Subreddit.

These are the basic tools that can help you with your journey as a beginning Amazon private label seller. You will find out what tools you *really* need as you start selling.

What are the costs involved in selling via Amazon FBA?

1. Sourcing the product

This is the initial cost that you need to cover because without products, you will not be able to start your business. The product cost depends on the number of units you want to order from the manufacturer. Since you are a beginner and you do not want to shell out tens of thousands of dollars right away, let's assume that you only want to order about 200 to 300 units of the product that you have in mind.

Wholesale orders usually run from $0.50 to $10 each unit. This is again dependent on the kind of product that you want to order. Let's say you want to order 300 units of canvas bags with fun prints and the price of each unit is $2 each. You have to pay $600 to the manufacturer. The cost of sourcing your product is less than $1000.

2. Shipping

You still need to do a little shipping even if you are selling via Amazon FBA. You need to ship the items to Amazon and you can use your own courier if you want to. Shipping fees depend on how you want the items to be shipped—by air or sea. Air cargo is more expensive than sea cargo, although air is much faster than sea. This is why people who want to expedite the delivery of something usually use air cargo. If your products have regular size and weight, the typical computation of the shipping fee is about 60% to 80% of the cost of the product. This percentage already includes the courier fees and the declared value of your items. Going back to the example in the previous point, if your manufactured products cost $600, your shipping cost would be around $360 to $480.

3. Branding and logo

This is an optional cost, but if you want your brand and logo to look professional, you might want to hire someone who can do it for you, unless of course you are good at doing such kinds of things. You can easily hire someone to work on your branding and logo on Fiverr. You just need to pay $5 (hence the name Fiverr). Aside from Fiverr, you can also search for freelancers on other sites (e.g. upwork). They can provide you with your logo and packaging design. Let's say you will spend around $50 for this.

4. Photography

Online selling requires great photos of your products because this is what your future customers will see. Although this is also an optional cost, having professionally done photos will make your products stand out among the rest. You will notice the difference when you browse through the different listings. It might be easier these days to take great photos even by just using your phone's camera but it is still a better idea to have professional-looking pictures.

These professionals know things than an amateur photographer might not know such as the right way to take pictures of certain items, lighting, and so on. Again, you can use the same website that you used for finding a freelance graphic designer. You might have 300 items but they are more or less the same so you do not really need to take a picture of each. Let's just say for all the photos that you need, maybe 10 different shots, you have to pay $100.

5. Online tools and software

These include product and keyword research tools, calculators, profit monitoring software, product tracking software, pricing tools, and so on. For beginners, you probably won't get all of these software tools at once. You will probably only get the one with the most features, say, Viral Launch. They offer different packages for beginners which cost $29, intermediate for $59, and pro for $99. If you decide to get the intermediate version like most sellers, you have to pay $59.

6. Inspection service

This is another optional cost because this depends on how much you trust your supplier. If your products are simple, like canvas bags, then hiring a company that provides inspection services is not necessary. But if your product is kind of complicated and the manufacturer is from abroad, you might want to have your products professionally inspected. This will cost you around $100 to $300.

7. UPC barcode

You can send a UPC barcode to the supplier so that you can have it printed on your products before they get sent out to Amazon. This will cost around $5.

8. Running ads

As a seller, you have the option to have your products sponsored. You can choose products and keywords that you want to appear for on Amazon's specific pages such as product detail pages and in search results. The cost of sponsored products and brands depends on how many times your ads get clicked. You can also set the budget that you want to spend for your ads. To give you an idea, the minimum daily budget for keyword targeted ads is $1.

9. Amazon costs

Amazon will not be doing all of these for free. There must be some fees involved. And you are right. In fact, Amazon sellers pay a lot of different fees for different purposes.

Product fees

There are three types of product fees that sellers pay to Amazon.

- Referral fee - 6% to 20%, average is 15%, based on category and selling price
- Minimum referral fee - $0-$2, if referral fee is smaller than minimum fee, based on category
- Variable closing fee- $1.80, for all media categories

To illustrate, let's say for instance you are selling 4 pieces of mugs for $5.99. The 15% referral fee would be $0.89 and the minimum fee for this category is $1. Since the referral fee of $0.89 is smaller than the minimum fee of $1, you will pay $1 to Amazon. Let's take another example. If you are selling a set of four fleece blankets for $24.99, your referral fee will be $3.75, which is bigger than the minimum fee of $1. In this example, you will pay the $3.75 referral fee.

Variable closing fee is a flat rate of $1.80 no matter how much the product costs. This will be added on top of the referral fee. Some examples of media categories where you have to pay variable closing fees are video games, video game consoles, software, music, DVD, and books.

Seller account fees

As discussed earlier, there are two types of seller accounts—individual and professional. Individual seller accounts have no monthly fees, but they have to pay a $0.99 listing fee when the item is sold. This account is ideal for occasional sellers. On the other hand, professional sellers, or those volume sellers and businesses, have to pay $39.99 per month, but they no longer need to pay $0.99 per listing.

Amazon FBA fees

The two major fees that you will pay if you decide to use FBA are:

- Fees for picking, packing, and shipping
- Monthly fees for storage (which means that the longer your products stay in the fulfillment centers, the higher your fees will be)

These fees are based on the size and weight of your products. They divide the product size into two categories—standard size and oversize. Any item with dimension less than 18"x14"x8" and weighs less than 20 pounds once packaged are considered standard-sized. Oversize products, on the other hand, are anything exceeding the dimension and weight mentioned above.

Amazon further divides each of these product size categories:

Standard-size:

- Small standard size that weighs 1 lb or less- $2.41
- Large standard size that weighs 1 lb or less- $3.19
- Large standard size that weighs 1 to 2 lbs- $4.71
- Large standard size that weighs over 2 lbs- $4.71 for first 2 lbs + $0.38 per additional lb

Oversize:

- Small oversize- $8.13 for first 2 lbs + $0.38 per additional lb
- Medium oversize- $9.44 for first 2 lbs + $0.38 per additional lb
- Large oversize- $73.18 for first 90 lbs + $0.79 per additional lb
- Special oversize- $137.32 for first 90 lbs + $0.91 per additional lb

The abovementioned fees include picking, packing, handling, shipping, customer service, and returns. Storage fees, on the other hand, are based on the volume of your inventory and the calendar months.

Standard size:

- Jan-Sept: $0.64 per cubic foot
- Oct-Dec: $2.35 per cubic foot

Oversize:

- Jan-Sept- $0.43 per cubic foot
- Oct-Dec- $1.15 per cubic foot

These are the basic fees that you need to know as an Amazon FBA seller.

Chapter 3

Product Research

Given that your product is the heart and soul of your business, it's very important you research what kind of products will sell well on Amazon. Here are some tips that you need to know when it comes to choosing the right product for your business.

Criteria for selecting a good product

1. Good demand

You have probably learned this in basic economics. For your business to flourish, there should be a good demand for the products you are selling. You have to understand that demand sells. One of the reasons why a product is not selling is because there is no demand for it, meaning people do not want or need it. Another is that you have overestimated its demand, which led you to overprice the product. Or maybe you are simply selling your products to the wrong market. Having a high demand for your products will surely lead to high sales. If you already bought your products and you realized later on that the demand for them is quite low, you can still do something about it by artificially creating a demand.

One way to create an artificial demand is through *exclusivity*. Ever wonder why Apple products are highly sought-after even if they are extremely expensive? One reason is exclusivity. For one, they are expensive, which means only people with that kind of money can afford them. Second, Apple does not release products left and right, unlike its competitors. Third, they have their own tech centers, app stores, and so on. This makes the owners of Apple products feel exclusive.

You cannot simply increase the price of your products, or sell them to certain groups of people. You can instead use other techniques, such as selling "limited edition" items. Or, you can sell certain items at a limited time only. This makes potential buyers think that your products are scarce, that if they don't buy one now, they might not have the chance to buy later. You can also offer incentives to first time buyers to increase demand.

2. Not too much competition

Finding a good product that has a high demand but does not have a lot of competitors is a dilemma that most sellers face. After all, if a product is in demand, a lot of business owners will surely want to sell them. Certain types of products such as clothing and shoes are already highly saturated by a lot of sellers.

You need to find a product that has a demand but does not have a lot of sellers that offer them. One such product is a niche product. There is probably a large group of people out there looking for certain types of products that typical businesses don't sell. For example, clothing is an in demand product, but there is too much competition. But, if you really want to sell clothes, you should find ways to tweak your product a bit to make it unique and original that will sell to a certain group of people. For example, you can sell vintage-style swimsuits instead of the regular swimsuits. You can also sell kinky outfits for couples who love to do role play sex.

These are under the clothing category, but you are targeting a niche. Another popular niche clothing product is vegan or sustainable clothes. You will still have competition, but it won't be too high as compared to mainstream types of clothes like what H & M or Forever21 sells.

3. Not too seasonal

Seasonal products are those that are in demand during a particular season such as Easter, Christmas, Fourth of July, Halloween, etc. Seasonal products are highly profitable if you are selling them at the right time. When they are no longer in season, these products will sit in the Amazon shelves for months, collecting dust and accumulating storage fees. This is why you should avoid buying a lot of seasonal products for reselling, such as decors, costumes, or treats. Do not spend thousands of dollars on these items because they will surely sit for a long time in storage. You can still buy seasonal products but only a limited amount and you should also know when you should start buying them – timing is critical.

If you really want to sell seasonal products, maybe you can sell something that will cover different seasons. For example, fairy lights can be a great Christmas décor, but they are also used by a lot of people as regular room décor. You can also sell generic gift baskets that can be given as gifts on Mother's Day, Christmas, graduation, and so on.

4. Affordable retail price

You might think selling high-priced items is the best way to go if you want to earn a high profit, but you are wrong because it is still best to choose products that you can sell at an affordable retail price. For example, if you decide to sell private labeled watches that have Swarovski crystals on them, this will cost you a lot of capital, which means that you have to sell them at an even higher price if you want to earn a profit.

People may not be willing to spend hundreds of dollars on a brand that they have not heard of. This is why you should sell affordable products as you are establishing your brand. Moreover, expensive items can sit for a long time in storage because people are generally more cautious when it comes to buying more expensive items. If you sell them products that will only cost them a few dollars, they will not even think twice, and just simply click the buy now button even if they don't really need it and without researching about it.

5. Fewer reviews

You might think that selling a product with a lot of reviews is a great idea because it means that a lot of people are buying them. Although this can be true, it also means that the market is highly saturated because there is already a lot of sellers selling the same product. A product with fewer reviews means that it does not have a lot of sellers yet. It is still an untapped market that has a lot of potential.

6. Room for improvement

Selling a perfect product may not be a great idea because it means that nothing else can be done with it. It is already the final and ultimate version of that product. No more improvement can be made, which means that the price remains the same. Although there is no such thing as a perfect product (after all, nothing is perfect in this world), there are still products that give you very little room for improvement.

The design or structure of the product is not something that you can tweak to modify. This is not a good kind of product to sell, especially for private label sellers because you cannot add any value to it to make it your own. You should choose a product that gives you a lot of wiggle room, a product that gives you enough space for creativity. In one of the examples given before, selling canvas bags is a good idea because it allows you to customize different designs and prints.

7. Not in gated categories

There are certain types of products that require sellers to get Amazon's permission before they can start selling them on the website. There is an approval process that sellers need to go through if they want to sell products under the gated category, which is why this is not a good product to sell on Amazon, especially for startups. Amazon has to "gate" certain items to protect their reputation, especially since the number of third-party sellers have increased dramatically over the last few years.

This is Amazon's way of protecting their reputation. They do not want to have counterfeit or low quality products being sold on their website. Some examples of gated categories are fine jewelry, DVDs, watches, grocery items and gourmet food, fine arts, collectibles, and automotive. During the holiday season, Amazon also gates toys and games.

8. Not likely to attract litigations

You should also choose products that are not likely to get you sued. First, you need to know the kinds of products that attract litigations. Some examples are food, vitamins, cosmetics, and anything that you put inside your body or apply on your skin or hair. If you want to avoid litigations, you better choose products that are not applied on the body, eaten, taken orally, or inserted inside the body.

Choose something easy and safe, such as canvas bags, pens, clothes, notebooks, blankets, and so on. There are thousands of products to choose from that are not likely to attract litigations. These types of products are for sellers or brands that are already established, such as Kylie Cosmetics or Hershey's. These are large corporations that have a team of lawyers handling these litigations. You, on the other hand, are a one-man team who is just starting and cannot afford (yet) to hire your own business lawyer.

9. Not too fragile

If you are a very patient person and money is not an issue, go ahead and sell products that easily break such as eyeglasses, ceramic mugs, plates, light bulbs, and so on. Selling these products can lead to a lot of returns because they get damaged easily, either during transit or while in storage. No matter how the product gets broken, you still have to process the return and refund or exchange and this is a lot to handle, especially if you are processing multiple return transactions. Just imagine if all of your products are easily breakable. You will probably spend more time and money processing returns than selling the product itself.

Five best selling categories on Amazon

Since you are planning to sell on Amazon, you should also know the best-selling categories on the website. This will give you an idea about the kinds of products that you can sell that will give you the highest sales volume and profits.

1. Books

It all started when Jeff Bezos, the founder of Amazon, started selling books online. This is why books are one of the top selling categories on Amazon. Books are Amazon's very first product category. We are not talking about digital books here. We are talking about the traditional kind made of paper and ink. You might think, are there still people reading physical books? Aren't there e-books that they can easily download on their Kindle and iPad? Yes, there are still a lot of readers who prefer paper books over e-books. This is why this is still a huge market. Moreover, books have a large profit margin.

You can buy books wholesale for just one dollar, give or take a few cents. And you know how much one paper book costs. You can mark up your book items at 1000% of the original price. Selling books on Amazon may not be something that you can consider as your major source of income, but it is definitely one of the most stable categories on Amazon that has a huge market, and will definitely give you a solid income regularly.

2. Workout clothes

These days, a lot of people enjoy doing physical activities — going to the gym, running, yoga, and so on. This makes exercise clothing one of the highest selling categories on Amazon. People want to be comfortable and at the same time look good while doing their favorite workout, especially since they take a picture of themselves wearing their exercise gear and post it on social media. In fact, the popularity of exercising and working out gave birth to a fashion trend called athleisure.

You will now see a lot of people wearing workout clothes not only in the gym or while exercising, but also when going to the grocery or even to parties. You see them wearing sports bra with leggings and running shoes everywhere. And despite the increasing number of people who buy second hand clothes, a lot of them still prefer brand new workout clothes. Nobody wants to wear a pair of used leggings or sports bra. It is a huge market right now, and you should definitely take advantage of that.

The only downside is that it is hard to find a manufacturer that can make high quality athleisure clothes. Low quality workout clothes are not comfortable to wear, and comfort is one of the things that you should look out for when it comes to buying workout clothes. You should also be aware of the characteristics of the workout clothes that you should be selling. There are clothes that absorb sweat or pull sweat away from the body. You also have to pick workout clothes for different physical activities and seasons.

3. Electronic items and accessories

For Amazon FBA sellers, electronic items might be difficult to sell because people would generally buy electronics from a well-established and known brand. What you can do instead is to just find electronic accessories to sell. You can sell a wide variety of accessories for different electronics— phone cases, laptop sleeves, laptop bags, phone pouches, power banks, memory cards, screen protectors, and so on. You can easily find a manufacturer for these. All you need to do is to find one that offers the best deal. There are a lot of different electronic devices that come out every few months and you can be sure that people will buy accessories for these.

However, having new devices come out every month is a double-edged sword. It is a positive thing for sellers because it means more things and varieties to sell for them. It is also a negative thing because devices get replaced fast, which means that you might still have some accessories for a device that is already obsolete. The key here is to monitor trends and do not buy too many items for one particular device.

4. Baby items

Baby items are always in demand because humans always procreate. And babies need a lot of stuff. In fact, they need more stuff than adults. Their stuff also get replaced fast because babies grow and develop fast, unlike an adult who can own and wear the same clothes for ten years. One advantage of selling baby items is that they are usually small and lightweight, unless of course you are selling baby furniture. They are also inexpensive, which can give you a huge profit margin. However, you should avoid selling baby items that can get you sued such as baby food or feeding supplies. Just stick with regular items like clothing, toys, blankets, and so on.

5. Clothing, shoes, and jewelry

These are always in demand anywhere you go. People always buy clothes, shoes, and jewelry. Workout clothes have a separate category because it has its own huge market. However, there is still a lot of people who buy regular clothes, and also shoes and jewelry. Please note that this does not include jewelry made of precious metals such as solid gold and expensive materials such as Swarovski. These are regulated products and might be difficult to sell.

Clothing, shoes, and jewelry have always had a huge market whether it is online or in physical stores. You can also buy them in bulk for dirt-cheap because there are already a lot of manufacturers to choose from. They are also easy to ship because of their small size. You can never go wrong selling them. The only drawback is that because they are a popular category, you will have a lot of competition. This is why you need to add something to your products that will make them stand out from the rest. Maybe you can focus on selling only one type of clothes, such as sleepwear or lingerie. For shoes, maybe you can sell foldable flat shoes that they can easily store in their bags. For jewelry pieces, you can sell vintage-inspired jewelry that are quite popular these days.

These are the things that you need to consider when it comes to selling products on Amazon FBA. Once you find the product that you want to sell after careful research, you can now proceed to finding a reliable manufacturer or supplier who can make these products for you or sell them to you wholesale.

Chapter 4

Sourcing the Product

You should now search for the manufacturer or supplier where you can get your products from. This can be intimidating for a lot of people, especially beginners because once you contact a supplier and order hundreds of units of an item, you can no longer back out or change your mind. You cannot simply say to the supplier that you do not want the items anymore after they started making them. You also cannot simply decide not to sell once you receive the products after spending hundreds or even thousands of dollars. What are you going to do with 100 pieces of baby clothes or 500 pieces of memo pads? Contacting a manufacturer signals the beginning of your business. You are already involving other groups of people, and you need to be professional about it.

Choosing a supplier may sound scary but it is not that difficult, especially today when everything is right at your fingertips. However, you should still be cautious because there are a lot of scammers out there, especially if you are ordering from abroad. To help you find and choose the right manufacturer or supplier for your business, here are some tips that you should know.

Where can you find suppliers?

These days, everything is made in China, and it is no wonder because there is a lot of manufacturers and suppliers of products in China. Although it is best to go to China and talk to the manufacturers in person, you can also simply contact them online. Here are some Chinese websites that you should check out.

https://www.alibaba.com/

This is probably the most popular website used by Amazon sellers. It is one of the biggest companies that do business with ecommerce sellers. Alibaba is based in China and has other websites—Tmall and Taobao. It is used by millions of people, including merchants, businesses, and individual sellers. Most of the people selling on Amazon get their products from Alibaba. Alibaba is like the yellow pages of manufacturers and suppliers. You will find here hundreds of companies that make products in bulk, usually by the hundreds. Their unit price is also dirt cheap, which gives you a chance to sell them at a higher mark up.

https://www.aliexpress.com/

Alibaba owns Aliexpress, and the two are not the same. The owner of Alibaba uses Aliexpress to compete against ecommerce giants such as Amazon and eBay. You can buy items per piece from

Aliexpress, but not from Alibaba. However, you can still source your inventory from Alibaba because they offer their products at factory prices in smaller quantities.

https://www.made-in-china.com/

Founded in 1998, Made-In-China is also one of the leading B2B ecommerce websites in China. It works the same way as Alibaba, by bridging the gap between Chinese suppliers and international sellers. It makes it easier for people all over the world to contact Chinese manufacturers.

Aside from Chinese suppliers, you can also find manufacturers and suppliers in the US and Europe, although pricing can be a little more expensive.

Here are some websites that you should check out.

http://www.zentrada.eu/

This website is one of the largest sourcing platforms used by ecommerce sellers in Europe. Individual sellers are given new ideas for ordinary products that help them to succeed. Currently, they have around 400 thousand units of different products that come from different manufacturers, importers, and wholesalers worldwide.

http://www.koleimports.com/

If you live in Los Angeles, California, you can try contacting Kole Imports, a family-owned business in the US. It is one of the biggest general merchandisers and direct importers of different consumer goods. Established in 1985, Kole Imports gets their products directly from manufacturers abroad, and sell them in bulk to retailers and wholesalers. You can visit their website by clicking the link above or you can go to trade shows where they are participating.

http://www.closeoutfortune.dollardays.com/

Also based in the US, Closeoutfortune offers wholesale products at a low price. They have a wide assortment of products to choose from, and they also have a wide range of customers — non-profit groups, retailers, e-sellers, and even schools. They are a great source of items to sell, especially for small businesses and non-profit organizations.

How to evaluate reliability of suppliers

The knee-jerk reaction for most people searching for a supplier is to choose the one that offers the lowest price. This should not be the case because the most important thing is to find a supplier who can deliver what they promised. If you find a reliable supplier, you won't have to keep searching for new suppliers every time you need to replenish your inventory.

1. Main product

When choosing a manufacturer for your product, you need to make sure that the product you want them to make is their main product and not just something that they sell on the side. For example, if you are planning to sell bed sheets, you should go directly to a manufacturer that makes bed sheets, instead of going to a manufacturer that sells mainly mattresses but also makes bed sheets on the side.

2. Main markets for exports

Manufacturers whose main target markets are businesses in developed countries are generally more reliable than those whose target are businesses in developing countries. This is understandable because developed countries have stricter policies when it comes to product quality and safety standards. They closely monitor defects and compliance to regulations imposed by different government bodies.

3. Compliance to product safety

You also need to choose manufacturers that comply with product safety standards. As a seller, it is your responsibility to ensure that your products are safe to use by the general public. Some product safety regulations that you should know as a seller are electrical safety regulations, product packaging regulations, toys and children's products regulations, textile regulations, and so on. You need to know what regulations your intended product to sell should adhere to. And then, you need to find a manufacturer that makes products that will pass such regulations with flying colors.

Compliance to such standards is critical when it comes to importing from overseas, especially China because it can lead to product recalls, fines, seized cargos, and even litigations. This might even cause you millions of dollars, especially if the damage caused by your product is fatal and serious.

4. Quality management system

Monitoring the quality of the products that a manufacturer makes is a must in any manufacturing company. They have to closely monitor their products during and after production to minimize the number of units with defects. The higher the number of defective units, the lower the sales will be. This also has a negative impact on the manufacturer's reputation, which is why they try hard to keep their defects at a minimum. You need to find a supplier that follows QMS or quality management system. Unfortunately, only a small percentage, about 5% to 10% of manufacturers follows QMS. To find them, they should have an ISO certificate, usually ISO 9001.

5. Transparency

Manufacturers who are not willing to undergo factory audit or quality inspection probably have something to hide. You can eliminate unreliable manufacturers by telling them early on that you are going to do quality inspections and testing of samples. If they refuse, you should not do business with them because a reliable supplier will be more than willing to have these inspections.

Criteria to use when evaluating a supplier

Your business has its own specific needs, and you need to make sure that you choose a supplier that meets these needs. You need to create a list of criteria that will help you choose the one that will be able to provide you with the kind of products and service that you are looking for.

1. Cultural fit

The manufacturer should uphold the same cultural value that your business stands for. For instance, if you want to sell items made from bamboo because you want to promote the use of sustainable products and at the same time earn money through your business, you should find a manufacturer who adheres to the same principles.

2. Cost

The cost of everything—from the production of the goods to shipping—should be within your budget. You need to find a manufacturer that can offer you the lowest cost per unit but still maintains the quality of the products that you are looking for.

3. Order quantities

This depends on how many you want to order. Most manufacturers have a minimum order requirement. If you are just starting, you might want to choose a supplier that allows you to order by the hundreds, say, 300 units of the item.

4. Follows safety standards and quality control systems

The company should follow all the required regulations in terms of safety and quality standards imposed by the country where you live. You can ask for certifications, ISO numbers, and other permits to ensure that you are dealing with a legitimate supplier.

5. Turnaround time

How long can the manufacturer finish the product? The faster the products are finished, the faster you can launch your business. However, make sure that the short turnaround time will not negatively affect the quality of the products.

6. Flexibility

They should be willing to adjust if there are changes to be made to the orders and the product itself, of course with necessary pricing adjustments.

These are just some of the things that you should consider when choosing a manufacturer or supplier to do business with. These should be laid out before you decide to search for suppliers to ensure that you are choosing the right one for your business needs.

How To Spot Shady Suppliers

Hopefully, in your journey as an online seller, you will never come across a shady supplier or a scammer who only wants your money. These shady suppliers can be avoided by knowing the signs that you are dealing with one. Here are the things that you should look out for.

1. Too good to be true

You always hear the saying if it is too good to be true, it's probably not true. This also applies when choosing a manufacturer. If they promise to move heaven and earth just to finish your product within a very short period of time, and they are working on low capital because the quote that they gave you is too low, then this is probably not legit. Low price does not always mean a great deal. You might be dealing with a scammer who just wants to attract people to scam by giving them unbelievable deals.

2. Too much self-promotion but no substance

When you contact the supplier because you are attracted by their rates, and you notice that the supplier talks too much about all the great things that they can give you but you do not really see a lot of positive reviews from previous customers, chances are they are just building themselves up to make you sign that deal. A legit supplier will ask questions about the work that you want them to do and will show you proof of successes from previous clients.

3. Quote is too generic

When you ask for a quote, they should be able to give you the breakdown of everything and how they arrived at that amount for you to understand what you are paying for. A shady supplier will probably give you a cookie-cutter quote that he got from Google.

4. Hidden fees

If the pricing that they give you is vague, which gives them an opportunity to change the price in the future, you should be wary because you are probably dealing with a shady supplier. If they say something like "you need to pay us around 600 dollars, but we're not sure yet about the kind of materials you want and we can only find out once we start to make the products after you make the payment", you should back off because this is not how it should be done. A legitimate seller will give you an exact amount to be paid. After all, they are supposed to have been doing this for years, so they should know by now how much they should be charging their clients.

5. Delays in communication

Delays in responding to your calls or messages can mean that the supplier does not have a designated department for handling questions of potential clients or is simply too busy or disorganized. Either way, you wouldn't want to communicate with such a seller because it shows unreliability. This might cause problems in the future when you need to talk to them urgently and no one is responding.

Ordering samples

One way to ensure that you are getting products that meet your standards is to ask for samples from the manufacturer.

Why order samples?

To test the quality.

Pictures are sometimes not enough because they can be misleading. If you have the sample in your hand, you will be able to see, smell, and feel the actual product that you are going to buy and later on sell to your future customers.

To test the supplier.

This is also a great way to test the supplier. You will know if they are willing to send a sample and you will also find out how they communicate and work with their clients. You will also see their packaging and how fast they process and ship their orders.

To let them know that you are serious.

This is a subtle way to let them know that you are serious about your orders. Suppliers also weed out hundreds of "buyers" that don't actually order anything. This will let them know that you are willing to go further if you are satisfied with the sample.

How many samples should you order?

Ideally, you should order one sample per product that you will be ordering. However, you have to consider your budget and shipping fees because if you have a lot of different products, you might want to limit your order to a few samples. Maybe if you are ordering everything from one manufacturer, you can order a couple of samples just to see if their real products are the same as the ones in their picture. Some manufacturers will also not buy materials and spend time and money on labor just to make one item. You have to consider different aspects and make sure that you ask your supplier how you should go about ordering samples.

Why hire an inspector to check the products before shipment?

Although you might need to pay extra if you hire a professional inspector, you will at least get professional inspection of the products that you are going to sell. This is also cost effective in the long run because you don't have to go to the supplier's factory in person just to check your orders. This also means lower return rates because products meet the quality standards. Hiring an inspector is also beneficial because they would know what to look out for. After all, it is their job and they are trained to spot defects and subpar quality products that an ordinary person might miss. And inspectors like these are usually located in the same country as the manufacturer, which means easier communication among the supplier, the inspector, and you because the inspector can act as an intermediary.

Searching for the right supplier is not difficult as long as you know where to look and what to look for and look out for. The next chapter will teach you how to ship the products once the manufacturers are done with your orders.

Chapter 5

Shipping the Products

Once the manufacturer has completed your orders, the next step is to have them all shipped to Amazon FBA warehouses. You need to research this part before you place an order, especially if you decide to source your product from Chinese manufacturers because there is a lot of processes involved when it comes to importing items from abroad.

For illustration purposes, let's assume that your manufacturer is from China, where most Amazon FBA sellers get their inventory.

Shipping from China to Amazon Warehouse

There are three ways to ship form China to Amazon Warehouse:
- The items will be sent directly to Amazon Warehouse from China.
- The items will be sent to your home first and then to Amazon Warehouse.
- The items will be sent to a third-party company and then to Amazon Warehouse. This company will also check and prep the products for you.

Chinese supplier - Amazon Warehouse

A lot of people use this first method because it is the fastest and cheapest way among the three options for obvious reasons. This is especially true if you decide to use air or express cargo. You have to pay for the shipping fee twice if the products have to go through your home or a third-party company.

Chinese supplier - You - Amazon Warehouse

Some sellers prefer that they see the products that they ordered first hand before selling them online. This is especially helpful when it comes to ensuring that the items meet Amazon's quality requirements. This is also ideal if you live near the US main ports, like Los Angeles. It will add more to your shipping expenses if you live far from major ports because of the additional transportation costs from the port to your home. However, if you do decide to have the items shipped to your home first, you will be responsible for prepping your products, which can be a tedious process, especially for beginners like you.

Chinese supplier - Third-party – Amazon Warehouse

If you want your products to be inspected, prepped, and monitored professionally, and you have extra money to spare, you can hire a third-party company that can do all these things for you. You need to find a third-party company that is also located in the same state as the Amazon FBA warehouse if you want to have low shipping costs. If it is located in a different state, the shipping costs will be a lot more expensive.

Shipping by sea or air

1. Sea freight

This is a complicated method of shipping items for export and import because it involves a lot of steps. It may be complicated but it is still one of the major ways to transport products from one country to another because it can accommodate a large shipment at a much lower cost. The main disadvantage is the length of time. Shipping by sea has several stages:

- From the Chinese supplier to Chinese port (domestic)
- From the Chinese port to the US port (international, export and import)
- From the US port to your home, to the third-party company, or directly to Amazon FBA warehouse (domestic)

Two forwarders are involved in the entire process — the Chinese and US forwarders. They have to coordinate with each other and handle all the processes involving importing and exporting these goods to and from their respective countries.

You can either find your own freight forwarder or you can let your supplier find one for you. You need to understand that Amazon is not responsible for anything related to customs clearance and does not provide any delivery support. They also do not act as a contact for overseas customs clearance. These are all the responsibilities of the freight forwarder and also the seller. If your goods do not meet the requirements of the customs, they will be detained and the freight forwarder should know how to handle such scenarios.

Finding your own freight forwarder vs. letting your supplier find one for you

If you think you will continue having this business for many years to come, you might want to find a freight forwarder that you can rely on. Sounds cheesy, but that's how it should be. Moreover, finding your own forwarder is beneficial because you can find someone who speaks the same language as you do. And you are satisfied with what you have researched about them. You can choose someone who meets all your business needs. You can choose either a freight forwarder who is located in China or in the US, although the former is preferred by many. The main reason is the ease of communication, as stated previously, and there will also be no time difference that can affect communication because you live in the same state.

If you find your own freight forwarder, your Chinese supplier should deduct the cost from the total amount that you have to pay. The amount depends on whether the forwarder will ship from the supplier's warehouse or from a seaport in China.

Most beginners usually resort to the second option of letting their supplier find a freight forwarder for them because they do not have a lot of contacts yet. But as they continue doing their business, they will get recommendations from fellow sellers on where to find the best freight forwarder. But you can still choose to let your supplier handle the shipment process. This is especially a great idea if your supplier has done business with an Amazon seller before because they already know how it works. You do not have to explain about Amazon fulfillment centers, and the right way to prep the products. Just make sure to ask about the shipping costs because sometimes, they do not include the cost of shipping from the US port to Amazon.

The benefit of letting your supplier find a freight forwarder for you is that you do not need to search for it. And searching for freight forwarders and knowing what questions to ask can be challenging. With the expertise and connections of your supplier, you can be sure that you will have a reliable freight forwarder who can handle your shipment for you. The only downside is that you are not learning the nitty gritty of processing shipments and searching for your own contacts because you let your supplier do it for you.

Cost of sea freight

As mentioned earlier, there are a lot of steps involved when it comes to shipping goods by sea. However, it is still the cheapest way to ship because it can accommodate a large volume of shipment, unlike air freight, which has a limit. The cost of sea freight depends on *where the shipment is coming from, where it is going and what month you are going to ship*. But for reference, you can use $300/CBM which includes all shipping costs from a seaport in China to one of Amazon's warehouses located in the south of the USA. This will at least give you a rough estimate of how much you will be paying. The United States is a large country, and the shipping costs also depend on where you are located in the US. If the Amazon warehouse is in the west coast, the shipping fee will be much lower than if it is located in the east coast.

There is also a minimum shipping capacity when using sea freight, which is 2-3 CBM per shipment. Keep in mind that when using sea cargo, most of the fees and charges that the freight forwarders need to pay in the entire process of importing and exporting the goods are fixed no matter how much CBM shipment you have. The minimum is 2-3 CBM which is not difficult to reach since you are shipping goods in bulk.

Shipping time

So how long does it take for your cargo to reach Amazon's warehouse from China if you use sea freight? There are so many factors involved that it usually takes at least 30 days for a shipment to reach Amazon's warehouse located in the west coast coming from a Chinese seaport. If the Amazon warehouse is located in the east coast, it will take an additional 10 days, so 40 days in total. This is the minimum timeframe, but it could take longer than that. For example, if you ship during the holiday season in the US or during a festival in China, your cargo might take a longer time. There are also times when the customs clearance takes a longer time to complete because they are processing a higher volume of cargos than usual. Other factors that can affect the delivery time are the weather, labor issues at seaports, seasonal behaviors, and so on.

Christmas is the best time to sell online because a lot of people are buying gifts for their loved ones. So if you are planning to sell stuff for Christmas, you have to make sure that your shipment leaves China by the last week of October. If not, you will suffer delays and your shipment that you intend to sell on Christmas will arrive late, probably after Christmas. During this time, there is a much higher volume of shipment, which is why things get stuck at the customs.

2. Air freight

The second method of shipping is via air freight, and this is ideal if your shipment exceeds 1000 lbs. If it is below 1000 lbs, you can try express cargo, which involves a courier company such as DHL, FedEx, and UPS. However, most sellers on Amazon use either sea cargo or air freight because they usually have a lot of stuff to ship. Just like with sea freight, goods shipped via air freight also have to go through customs clearance. And just like sea freight, you also need to find a freight forwarder who will handle the entire process, including clearing customs. You have to make it clear to your freight forwarder that you want to pay for the total cost of shipping the products. You do not want to pay fees again when the shipment reaches your home or for import and export fees. This should be clarified by the freight forwarder before you decide to use their service.

Cost of air freight

When it comes to air freight shipping, the cost depends largely on the weight and volume of your shipment. Typically, air freight shippers charge per dimensional weight or actual weight, depending on which one is higher. To calculate the dimensional weight, you need to multiply the shipment's volume in CBM by 167. For example, if your shipment has a dimension of width-60 cm x height- 60 cm x length- 60 cm, you will get 216,000. Divide this by one million and you will get 0.216. To get the volumetric weight, multiply this by 167. Your shipment's volumetric weight is 36.072 kgs. If this is bigger than the shipment's actual weight, you will be charged based on the volumetric weight, or vice versa.

Compared to sea freight, air freight is a lot more expensive, especially if you are shipping heavy items. Imagine if you are shipping items that weigh a total of 2000 lbs in a medium sized box by sea from Shenzhen, China to New York, USA, you only have to pay $1200. But if you ship the same item via air freight to and from the same destination, you have to pay a whopping $4000.

Shipping time

Obviously, shipping via air freight takes a much shorter time than sea freight because airplanes are 30 times faster than ships. It will only take your shipment 3 days to one week, again depending on different factors such as speed of getting cleared at the customs, holiday season, and so on. This is why air freight is a lot more expensive than sea freight.

If you are pressed for time, you should consider choosing air freight. Maybe you are planning to sell before the holiday rush and you want your items to reach on time. Or maybe you are selling goods that have expiry dates or items that are seasonal. Electronics and other expensive items are also usually shipped via air because they will have a lower chance of getting lost or damaged because of the shorter shipping time. They are also more protected in planes than in ships in terms of storage conditions.

CO2 emissions

You already know that airplanes emit a large amount of CO_2 in the air. And if your business values sustainability, you might want to consider shipping via sea freight. According to a research conducted by the UK government, an ocean liner carrying 2 tonnes of shipment for 5000 km will only have 150 kgs of CO_2 emissions. Compare this to 6605 kgs CO_2 emissions of an airplane carrying the same load and traveling the same distance, choosing sea freight over air freight will seem like a no-brainer for people who are pro-environment and sustainability.

Import duty of products and other taxes

You also need to know the different fees involved in shipping your items. It is not just the cost of the service provided by the freight forwarder. They also have to pay different fees and taxes throughout the whole process. Import duty and taxes are calculated based on customs value and category of goods or HS code.

Customs value

Ideally, the customs value is calculated as: cost of product + cost of transportation to the Chinese port + export clearance in China. However, freight forwarders just estimate the amount at 20% to 30% of the value of the product in the United States, and this is what they declare at the customs clearance. To estimate the tariff of the product, you just multiply this amount to the current tariff rate.

HS code

Customs also assigns a standardized classification system to determine customs duty. HS Code means Harmonized Commodity Description and Coding System or simple Harmonized System. This consists of classification names and numbers to sort out traded goods that come in and go out of the country. You have to ensure that you assigned the correct HS code to your goods. Otherwise, you may be charged the incorrect customs duty.

Since you are not shipping the goods yourself, you do not really have to worry about these things because the freight forwarder or the courier company handles the entire process from start to finish. All you have to do is to be aware of these details so that you at least have an idea how much you need to pay when shipping your products. Once your products are shipped, or even before they reach their destination, you can now start preparing the products for sale by creating and building your brand.

Chapter 6

Preparing the Product for Sale by Branding

After receiving your items or even before receiving them, you need to prepare your products for sale by creating and building a brand. Your brand is a lot more than the name and logo of your business. It is the complete package—your products, business model, methods of advertising, values, and customer experience. This is why building a good brand is just as important as having a good product to sell.

Building a brand that is sustainable

These days, the more popular meaning of sustainability is being green and eco-friendly. And this is something that a lot of companies should strive for because more and more consumers are becoming more aware of the impact of their consumption to the environment. Another meaning of sustainability in terms of branding is lasting for a long time and remaining relevant for many years. This is also something that your business branding should aim for. You have to make sure that your branding is not just a fad or a trend. It should be sustainable and last for a long time to ensure that you have continuous business.

Choose a product that allows you to add other related products

When it comes to choosing a product to sell, you have to make sure that it allows you to add other related products as time progresses. And choose a brand that does not only focus on your specific product. For example, if you are selling quirky notebooks and your branding is something like All Quirky Notebooks, people will automatically assume that you are only selling fun notebooks with quirky designs. Sure, maybe you can add other related products like memo pads or pens and pencils, but that's about it.

What you can do is to change your branding into something more inclusive, like All Things Quirky so that you can add other related products later on as long as they have a quirky design. Another great example of this is selling electronic devices. Mobile phones, for instance, have different kinds of accessories such as cases, screen protectors, chargers, power banks, and so on. By selling complementary products, you will retain regular customers because they will not go somewhere else to look for accessories or other related products and you will also attract new customers who want to buy your other items.

Continuously create a need for your products

To keep your products' relevance in the market, you should continuously create a need for your products that will make people want to buy them. One way to do this is by promoting exclusivity of your products. For example, you can offer your products as limited editions that will make people think that they will not be sold after a particular time. You can also make your products or your promotion available only to a specific group of people. For instance, you can offer your discount or a specific product only to your Amazon customers and not to people who buy them from your physical store or other online selling platforms. This will create a need for your products that can make your business more sustainable.

What you need to know about trademarks

You always hear the word trademark but what does the word really mean? It is sometimes used interchangeably with branding which is the representation of the company. It could be a symbol, logo, phrase, or word that a company uses. Basically, a business needs a trademark to protect its intellectual property. To make your business qualified for trademark, you have to make sure that you use the brand for commercial purposes and the brand must be unique to your business.

There are certain things in your company that you can trademark such as unique names of your products and business, the words or phrases that you use for your products or marketing campaigns, symbols and logos that your company uses, and so on. You can even trademark scents, colors, and sounds that are unique to your brand and you do not want other people to use without your consent.

Types of marks

When it comes to name branding, there are four types of marks that you should know

- Descriptive,
- Suggestive,
- Arbitrary, and fanciful.

Descriptive mark is anything that has acquired a secondary meaning. For example, if you want to name your business after your last name which is McDonald's, say, McDonald's Cakes and Pastries, you will not be allowed to do so because McDonald's already acquired a secondary meaning as an American fast food chain. The most commonly used trademark is the suggestive mark. It does not entirely describe the company or the product but it gives consumers a hint of the kind of products that the company sells.

Some examples of suggestive brands are Netflix, Airbus, and Citibank. The third kind of mark is the arbitrary marking, which is a word, or phrase that has nothing to do with the company or products that they sell. One example is Apple. Apple does not sell the fruit apples but mobile phones, laptops, and computers. Windows is another great example of arbitrary trademark. Finally, fanciful marks are any original terms created for your specific business or product, such as Kodak, Aveeno, Exxon, Pepsi, and Polaroid.

Why do you need trademarks?

As mentioned before, trademarks protect your business from intellectual property theft. It also allows you to set your company and your products apart from other similar businesses to prevent confusion. Trademarks also prevent unfair competition such as imitation, trademark infringement, and use of other company's confidential information or trade secrets. Having a trademark also allows consumers to buy with confidence, knowing that the brand they are buying from is known for selling quality products.

Trademarks also allow consumers to know where the products come from in terms of the sponsor, the manufacturer, and the seller. When you apply a trademark for your business, you have to renew it after 10 years. And if you continuously use your products for five years, you can apply for incontestable status, which will give your business better rights to ownership and better protection against infringement.

Having your own trademark gives you exclusive rights to use the branding in your business. If you find other businesses using your trademark, you can pursue legal action against them because you were given the right to use that branding exclusively for your business.

Should startups register a trademark?

Some people think that trademarks are only used by large corporations such as Coca Cola or Microsoft and startups/small businesses do not really need them. This kind of thinking is the reason why some people end up losing their business. They do not anticipate these kinds of things, thinking that their business will not become as big as these corporation giants. You need to think ahead if you want your business to succeed.

It is best to protect your business from the start, especially if you have a unique branding and if your products are one-of-a-kind. This will allow you to take legal actions if your business' intellectual property rights are violated in the future. The bottom line is that you also need to trademark your brand if you want to protect your business from potential intellectual property theft in the future.

To illustrate the importance of acquiring a trademark for your brand, let's take a look at this made-up scenario. Emily started selling clothes that she designed herself in her neighborhood that she calls New Threads. She didn't bother to get a trademark for her business because she thought it was just a small business and nothing would really come out of it on a larger scale.
After some time, she noticed that a competitor in a different neighborhood who is also selling clothes also uses the same name. This case is still easy to handle because it's in a small area. As

long as Emily can prove that she started using the name before her competitor, she can continue using the brand for her business.

The problem will be much more complicated if there is another competitor in a neighboring state that uses the same name and who already filed an application for a federal trademark for the name New Threads. Emily might still have the right to use the name in the area where she loves, but she can't really sell interstate because another company has already trademarked the name, which means that Emily has to change her business name if she wants to expand her business outside her town.

This could have been avoided if she filed a trademark from when she started the business. She could have chosen a different name for her business because another company is already using it. Or if she is the first one to use the name, she will have all the rights to the brand and the competitor will not be allowed to use that name in the first place. And if Emily is going to change her name to be able to sell to other states, she might lose customers because some of them might not know that it is the same company.

This is why it is best to trademark anything related to your business that could potentially cause intellectual property lawsuits and claims in the future. However, you have to make sure that you have finalized your branding before you consider filing for a trademark. Maybe in the beginning, you are still unsure about the name and logo of your business and you might still want to do some small changes to them. The most important thing to remember is to file as early as you can once you are sure about the kind of branding that you want your business to carry.

Perform a trademark search

Once you have decided to have your name or logo trademarked, the first thing that you need to do is to conduct a trademark search. You need to understand that just because your trademark application was approved, that does not mean that no other company is using it. As a business owner, it is your responsibility to find out if someone else has already used the name you chose for your business. This means that a company who owns the trademark to the name that you are both using has all the right to take a legal action against you. If the other company wins the case, you need to stop operating your business under that name.

You can do a personal search online, which is relatively easy and inexpensive. This will not be your final search but is just a preliminary search that will filter out a lot of names that have already been trademarked. You can conduct your own trademark search by going to the following websites:

- http://www.wipo.int/branddb/en/
- https://www.tmdn.org/tmview/welcome
- http://tsdr.uspto.gov/
- https://igerent.com/trademarkstudy

Aside from conducting your own trademark search, you can also seek the help of a professional. Be sure that the searches that these companies perform include not only state registered marks but also federal. And you shouldn't just be searching for registered trademarks. You also have to make sure that you also search unregistered trademarks. Although you will have a bigger chance at winning a case against a company who hasn't registered their name, you still wouldn't want to experience the hassle of proving that you own the rights to your brand.

How much does it cost to register a trademark?

You can go about this in two different ways. The first one is to file the application yourself either online or on paper. You can submit your trademark application via an online service or using TEAS or Trademark Electronic Application System. The fees for applying online can range from $225 to $400 per class of services or goods. If you decide to go via the paper route, you need to pay $600 per class of services or goods. The more types of products or services you are planning to sell under that name, the more trademark fees you have to pay. Keep in mind that the fees are non-refundable even if your application to register the trademark was rejected.

The second way to register a trademark is by hiring a lawyer. Depending on the lawyer, you may need to pay around $125 per hour or more, or a flat fee decided by the lawyer.
As stated previously, you need to renew your trademark application every ten years, which will cost you $300 if you do it online, or $400 if you submit a paper application.

Now that your products are ready, you now need to launch your products to the public. You can check out the next chapter that will talk about the step-by-step process on how to do a product launch.

Chapter 7

Product Launch

Conducting a product launch is important if you want to let people know about your products and business. A product release is different from a product launch. A product release is just a company releasing a new product and announcing it to the public. A product launch is more fun and exciting, and usually creates buzz and stirs interests among the general public. A product launch is not just something internet marketers do. Everyone who has target customers or audience can do a product launch and will benefit from it, especially startups like your business.

Reasons for doing a product launch

Create a cash windfall

For those who do not know, a cash windfall is a sudden increase of income due to a single event, such as a product launch. One popular example is Apple's product launch of their latest iPhone. Their product launch was extremely successful because people lined up to different stores all over the world to be one of the very first ones to own the new iPhone. Apple experienced a spike in sales several days after the launch of the product because they were able to create hype around their latest gadget for sale, and people participated in the hype and bought iPhones within a few days after its initial release. If your product launch is successful, you will also experience a cash windfall.

Leave a lasting impact

Although the main objective of starting a business is to earn money, you should also want to leave a lasting impact on others, especially the people who patronize your product. You can achieve this if you do a product launch. If you conduct a product launch for your goods made of bamboo, you will be known as that startup company that sells sustainable and eco-friendly products made of bamboo.

Achieve strategic positioning

Conducting a product launch also helps you properly position your business and your products in the market. There is already a lot of businesses selling things made of bamboo, so how can you position your business in such a way that you are not just another business selling bamboo products? You need to make sure that in your product launch, you position your products using the superlative—the "most affordable", the "most sustainable", etc.

Gain more customers

If you don't have a product launch for your business, only a few people will know about your business—your family, your friends, your family's friends, your friends' friends, etc. But if you have a product launch, more people will hear and know about you, even those people whom you are not connected with in any way will know about your product. And the more people know about your business and products, the higher your sales potential will be.

Establish your authority

Businesses that have product launches are most often considered the authority in the industry. This is because they are more visible to the general public. Anything that is more visible to the eyes of the public is more likely to have a bigger influence over them. And you can achieve visibility for your business by doing a product launch.

Open doors

Product launches are not only done for your intended customers. Other people who may help you with your business such as other owners of startups, influencers, manufacturers, and so on will also hear about your products. This can also help you build your network or connections that can help you get ahead in your chosen industry.

How to do a successful product launch?

Run Facebook Ads

Many successful Amazon sellers use Facebook Ads to boost their rankings on Amazon and also to increase sales, while at the same time creating a network of audience that consists of fans who cannot get enough of your products. Running Facebook Ads is one of the most cost-efficient sources of traffic outside your online selling platform, in this case, Amazon. It is no wonder because there are over 2 billion people who actively use Facebook every month. Facebook Ads are shown to people who are interested in your product or anything related to it. And these same people will most likely be converted as your buyers.

One important thing that you should do is to create a landing page. Do not make the mistake of most sellers who lead traffic directly to their Amazon products. Remember that people who are browsing on Facebook are not looking to buy anything. Besides, there is no way for you to collect your potential customers' contact information if you direct them to your Amazon listing right away. A landing page can do this for you. If you can't capture their email address and they don't buy from you, you will no longer have any way to contact them in the future to make them interested again in buying your product.

Basically, the route of a customer that comes from Facebook should look like this:

Facebook → Landing Page (capture email, send promo code) → Amazon (sale).

Split testing is also a must when it comes to running ads on Facebook. It is creating different versions of your ad based on your target audience. If you are selling clothes and you have two kinds of audience, one is a mother and the other is an unmarried female, you should use two different pictures or copy according to their different needs. A mother will most likely click on wholesome and practical pictures while a single female will be more interested in something fun and flirty. I go into a lot more details in my book Facebook Advertising – Your Step by Step Guide To Generating Quality Leads For Your Business At a Very Affordable Cost

Create a Facebook fan group

This one is quite popular. If you are an active user of Facebook, you are most likely a member of at least one Facebook group. If you live under a rock and you have no idea what a Facebook group is, it is a page on Facebook regarding a certain topic or interest where a group of people join and interact with each other. There are Facebook groups for people who love to crochet, for people who love Ariana Grande, and so on. You can also create a Facebook group for your business. This allows you to network, recruit brand ambassadors, establish relationships with customers, support customers who need assistance, and create a community for your business.

Run Amazon ads

The first step that you need to do to run Amazon ads is to create a campaign. Just select a product that you want to advertise, set a budget, and decide on the length of your campaign. For instance, you can set a $10 budget per day and not set any end date for your campaign so that Amazon users can see your ad anytime. You can either choose automatic or manual targeting that allows you to pick keywords for your products. Automatic targeting is best for beginners. Once you have completed the setup, your sponsored products will be launched immediately. Your ads will then be shown to customers who are searching for your products or related items. When they click on your sponsored product ad, they will be directed to your product listing where they can read the product details and information.

Build an email list

This is one of the key elements of modern marketing. An email list is a collection of your visitors' and customers' email addresses that you can use for marketing. You can send promotions, news, and updates about your business via email to your existing and potential customers. You cannot just randomly ask people for their email address because that will look a little scam-y. You need to use effective and subtle strategies that will make people give you their email address. One way to do this is to create a personalized CTA or call-to-action for your landing page, blogs, or any write up about your business.

A CTA is something that a visitor of the page has to do, such as "Click on this link to answer a free quiz" or something like that, and then they will be asked to enter their email address to see the results. Product launches are also a great way to get email addresses. You can ask all participants to leave their contact information to register. You can also ask them to register on your website if they want to learn more about your products. Conducting contests, raffles, and giveaways on different social media platforms or during your product launch is also a great way to build your email list.

Do giveaways

There are different ways to do a giveaway. One way to do this is by posting your giveaway event on your Facebook page or group and asking your members or followers to join by simply typing in their email address, tagging their friends, and sharing your page. This is also a way to build your email list. You can also do it by sending out details of your giveaways to your email list. There is also a lot of websites that you can use to promote your contests and giveaways for free such as the ones below:

- http://www.giveawaymonkey.com/submit-giveaway/
- https://www.theprizefinder.com/upload-competitions
- http://juliesfreebies.com/giveaway-submission-form/
- http://giveawayfrenzy.com/giveaway-submit/
- http://www.totallyfreestuff.com/submit.asp?m=13

All you need to do is to provide the details of your giveaway or contest and once they are live on these sites, you can share them on your Facebook page and group, Instagram page, blogs, and other online platforms.

Get reviews

One reason why you want to conduct a product launch is to let people know about your product and get reviews from them. Having reviews, especially positive ones, is beneficial because people are more confident to buy a product that has a lot of positive reviews. Selling great products is already a given if you want to get positive feedbacks from your customers. But to get them to review your product in the first place is the challenging part. What you can do is to send an email requesting reviews or feedbacks to your email list.

You can also ask your Facebook community to write reviews and leave a rating after using your product. Amazon also offers the Early Reviewer Program for new sellers because they know how difficult it is to obtain a review from your first time buyers. For a fee of $60 per SKU, Amazon will send an email to those who have already bought your product, offering them an incentive of up to

$3 for writing a review. To be eligible, you have to be a registered seller in the U.S. and your product should cost at least $15 and up and has less than five reviews at the moment.

Choosing the right photographer for your product

For your product launch or your business in general to be successful, you need to have high quality pictures that will encourage people to buy your products. The picture should not only be clear but also accurate and honest. You may have a good DSLR camera, but if you are not a professional photographer, the pictures may still not look quite as good as what you see online. This is why it is better to hire someone who can take professional pictures of your products. You may need to pay extra but at least, your pictures will look amazing.

To choose a photographer, here are the things that you need to consider.

1. Portfolio.

Professional photographers should have a portfolio where you can see their past works and projects with different clients. You will know if their photography style suits your needs. It is best to choose a photographer who has already worked with online sellers previously because they know what needs to be done.

2. Experience.

Ideally, you should hire a photographer that has at least three years of experience taking pictures professionally. Hiring a newbie may be the cheapest option, but it can be risky because you have no idea how they work and what kind of photos they can create.

3. References.

Asking for references is a good way to know more about the photographer from a past client's perspective. You can ask about the photographer's work ethics, honesty, professionalism, and quality of output.

4. Pricing.

Be sure to ask about the pricing before you make any commitment. The pricing should be clarified in advance so that there will be no misunderstanding or surprise expenses in the future. You can either pay per image or per package deal, depending on how many pictures you need.

5. Communication.

The photographer should also be easy to contact. You might have some specific styles in mind and details that you want to highlight about the product, and these are things that you should tell the photographer. You should have the photographer's email address and phone number in case you need to ask or tell them something.

6. Free trial.

You can also ask for a free trial before you decide to hire the photographer's services. This is a great way to learn more about the photographer's creative style and work ethics.

Optimizing product listings to boost sales

If you want to improve the ranking of your Amazon listing that will make your product more visible to Amazon users, which in turn will increase your sales, you need to know how to optimize your product listing. Amazon product optimization is one of the best things that you can do for your business. There are different ways to do this.

Optimizing keywords

You already know how this works. The use of good keywords is the key to the success of your online business. Put yourself in the shoes of your target customer. If you are planning to buy, say, Disney bed sheets, you will definitely type Disney bed sheets in the search field. As a seller, you should use Disney bed sheets as your keywords. But you can also use additional keywords such as Aladdin bed sheets (or whichever Disney character you have), Disney bedding, Disney bed linen, and so on. These are the relevant keywords for the product that you are selling. If you just put bed sheet in your product listing without the word Disney, your item will not appear when a customer looking for Disney bed sheets searches for the product specifically. Here are some things that you should know when creating your listing:

- Your product title should include the top five keywords.
- You should add generic keywords (or backend keywords) aside from your most relevant keywords that do not exceed 249 bytes.
- You can use keywords in your product description and bullet lists, but make sure that the sentences still flow naturally.
- You can also add keywords (men/women) to make sure that you reach your target buyers.

Optimizing the content

Keyword optimization ensures that your product appears in the search results when the customer types relevant and related keywords. Optimizing your content, on the other hand, will make your target customer click on your listing. To improve your content, you need to focus on these three important points:

- Product information,
- Product texts and
- Images.

Product text and information overlap because they are both about the write up or description of the product. Product information is about the details that a buyer needs to know about the product such as the dimension, weight, material used, features, and so on. The advantages or benefits should also be included. The product text, on the other hand, is the way you present it to the customer. All these details and information should be presented in such a way that they are easy to read and understand. You can present some of the information in bullet points and be sure to be as straightforward and concise as possible.

The images that you use for your product listing should also be optimized. After all, this is the first thing that the customers see in the search results. You need to post one main image and additional images. The main image should show the core product as clearly as possible. It should have a white background and occupy 85% of the image frame. You can add more pictures for the accessories, packaging, demonstrative graphics, important features, environments, and so on.

Avoid duplicate content

One common mistake that online sellers make is using the same content in all their online selling platforms. Duplicate content is a big no-no because search engines will see this and think that you are copying content when both are just written by the same person—you. You should use a different write up for your Amazon listings, a different one for your own website, and so on.

Anatomy of a product listing

a) Product title

Amazon gives you a 250-character limit or about 50 words to write your product title. You need to use it wisely by making sure that all the words are important. When writing the product title, you have to keep in mind that you are writing for humans, not robots. Amazon may be using algorithms but these algorithms are still based on the search patterns and behaviors of humans. *You should also consider adding at least one key element or a benefit that sets your product apart from the products sold by your competitors.* For example, you can add keywords like biodegradable or eco-friendly. And remember that the keywords that you put in the title are more important than the words in the description because this is what the algorithm is looking into, so choose your words carefully. Make sure the keywords in your title are relevant to your product.

b) Product photos

Amazon allows you to upload up to 9 photos and you should definitely use all of them. When people scroll through the results of their searches, the first thing that they look at is the image, then the title. They will only click on the listing if they find the image and the title interesting. This is why you have to make sure that your image catches the attention of your target buyers. Your main image should have a white background and should be 85% of the entire frame. In the remaining pictures, you can show different angles of the product, zoomed parts, the packaging, and so on.

c) Important features

The character limit of this part of your listing is around 240 words or 1000 characters. It is best to write a bulleted list because no one likes reading a text heavy paragraph. You should have at least five bullets and *the most important features should be at the very top of the list.*

d) Description

This is where you can write in sentences but you should still make sure that your paragraphs are not too long. You can elaborate on the features that you already have in your bulleted list and add more important details about the product. The limit is 2000 characters including spaces, which is about 300 words.

Amazon Advertising (AA)

Amazon Advertising (formally called Amazon Marketing Services, AMS) is a system or a set of online tools that help sellers drive traffic to their listings. This was touched briefly while discussing how to run ads on Amazon and you already know that there are two types—automatic and manual. Basically, manual targeting depends a lot on you as the seller. You have to do some research and define your target keywords yourself. Automatic AA, on the other hand, is much simpler and easier because you leave everything to Amazon. All you have to do is to set it up.

Whether you are using manual or automatic, you can still get the same kinds of benefits. The first one is that you improve your visibility to potential customers by improving your ranking using relevant keywords. It also helps increase your sales at a faster rate, which makes Amazon more willing to promote your products. After all, Amazon will be more than happy to help sellers who have fast moving items.

Using AA ads search report to your advantage

Did you know that you can check how well your keywords performed in the actual searches? All you need to do is to download the data that will give you valuable insight about your keywords.

You can pull out account-level data and also choose dates that you want to study in the past 90 days. This way, you will see what makes your campaigns successful or not. For example, if you see a significant increase in sales in the past two weeks, you can pull out the data from that time frame and check out how customers reached your listings in terms of the keywords that they used. You can also determine which keywords do not work. This way, you can use the effective keywords and discard the ineffective ones in your future listings.

Testing different price points

Pricing is not as easy as adding a few dollars to the original cost to earn a profit. There are so many other factors that affect pricing and have nothing to do with how much has been spent making the product. The demand, for instance, hikes up the price. Just look at hotel rates and airfare. The price of your product also will dictate its perceived value. For instance, if you are selling a pen for a dollar, people will think it is just an ordinary pen. But if you are selling it for $100, people will think that there must be something special about that pen. And of course it should have something special about it. Maybe it is gold-plated or it was a designer pen. You cannot simply increase the price without a valid reason to do so. The price of your product gives people an idea about the quality. So be sure that your product meets their expectation.

To decide on your products' pricing point, you need to conduct a competition analysis. This means that you have to research on your competitors' prices. How much are they selling the same product? Are people buying them? This is important, especially if there is a lot of other vendors selling the same thing. It is difficult to increase your price because buyers will surely pick the cheaper option if the items are just identical.

You can either sell something unique which no one has ever sold before so that you can dictate the pricing of the product in the market. Or you can add value to your product and make it stand out. You can also do some simple manipulations such as using a different picture or name. If you find in your research that the same product that you are selling range from $5 to $10, you might want to price yours at $7. People will not go to the cheapest one because they will think there is a catch or maybe the quality is too low. They will also not buy the expensive one because they can find cheaper options. They will surely go for the mid-priced item because it meets all their needs.

You can also try split testing on Amazon. You can do this by tweaking certain parts of your listing to know which ones give you the highest sales. You can change the product title, the bullet points in your product description, the images, and of course, the price. For example, on the first couple of months, you can set the price of your pen at $1 each. The next couple of months, you can change the price at $1.50 each. After conducting your split testing, check which period gives you the highest number of sales.

When doing split testing, you should be patient because it may not tell you anything right away, especially if you are not making a lot of sales. If you only have one or two sales, you do not have enough data to work with. You should also avoid running too many tests at once because it will be hard to know what's working and what's not.

Remember that the price of the product is one of the major factors that help consumers decide what product to buy. This is why you have to choose the right pricing point for your goods.

Chapter 8

What Comes Next?

Having a successful launch does not ensure a successful business. It is just the beginning because you still have a lot of things to do. As they say, your product launch is just the beginning of your marketing journey. It's not the end goal. Pat yourself and your team (if you have one) on the back for a successful launch. Go home and enjoy your success. But afterwards, you still need to do something to maintain the success that you achieved on your product launch.

A successful product launch should touch on the first three levels of the marketing funnel.

- **Reach** - Getting your business message across to your target audience.
- **Attract** - Getting your target audience to check out your website, which will turn them into leads.
- **Convert** - Turn these leads into customers and getting them to sign up to your website and receive news and updates.
- **Educate** - Teach customers everything they need to know about your product and business to make them love your product even more.

Product launches significantly increase the volume of traffic to your website, which means that you achieve the "reach" and "attract" part of the marketing funnel. But for your launch to be considered successful, you should also have a high conversion rate, which means that people who receive your message and visit your website also sign up and buy something.

But to have consistently high sales, you need to reach the fourth stage, and that is to continuously educate your existing customers about your product to make them love your product and not buy anywhere else. You can do this by sending them news and updates about your products and ongoing promotions through email. You can also make them feel appreciated by giving them discounts and freebies.

Analyze post-launch feedbacks

A successful product launch results in people buying your products. But what about those who don't? What keeps them from buying your product? To know the answer to these questions, you need to analyze the feedbacks you receive after the launch. You probably have expectations as regards your target audience and the reasons why they are going to buy your product. These are just assumptions, which will only become clearer once you get their unfiltered feedbacks. Listen to the different feedbacks of people who buy your products and people who don't, and analyze the reasons behind their actions.

You need to analyze both quantitative and qualitative data. Quantitative data could include the number of people who give you a feedback, the number of people who participate in your launch, the number of people who give you a positive or negative feedback, the number of converted leads, and so on. Qualitative data, on the other hand, involves the content of their feedbacks. Analyze the words and phrases that they use. If the words "expensive" always comes up, it could mean that they find your products expensive which keeps them from making a purchase.

Improve the product

The act of selling a better version of a product is called upselling. To continuously satisfy your existing customers and to attract new ones, you need to make sure that your products continuously evolve for the better. To do this, you need to understand the product you are selling. What makes customers buy your products? What are the key selling features of your products? On the other hand, what are the weak spots of your product? You can find out the answers to these questions by reading customer feedbacks. To make product improvements, you can either add new features or improve existing features.

If you decide to add a new feature, be sure that it is something that will add value to your product and the customers will be happy about. Adding a new feature often creates a big marketing splash because people are excited to hear about changes to something that they already know. Outsiders will also hear about the new feature and will become curious, and might end up buying the product just out of curiosity. Adding new features may be risky, but it can also be highly rewarding if done correctly.

Improving on an existing product feature is a safer route to take, and you can do it in three different ways. The first one is deliberate improvement in which you improve on a feature so that the product works much better. The second one is frequency improvement wherein you improve a product feature so that the consumer will use it more often. And the third one is adoption improvement where the change leads to an increase in the number of people who are using the product.

Making changes on a product is a great way to maintain sales, but make sure that you are not adding unnecessary features or making unnecessary changes. Remember the saying "if it ain't broke, don't fix it"? This also applies to product improvement. This is especially true if you already have a large group of customers who have been using your product and are satisfied with it. What you can do is to create new products, which leads us to the next point.

Create new products

This is also a great way to attract more customers and make existing customers buy more. By adding new products to your already existing ones, you are reaching out to a larger group of people while at the same time not losing your loyal customers. If you simply add or improve a feature, there is a bigger chance of losing existing customers who are not happy about the change. If you simply create a new product and add it to your store, you will only attract new customers and also give more options to your existing customers. For example, if you are selling unscented shampoo bars, you can create new products with different scents and continue selling your unscented ones because these already have a loyal following. There is no reason to stop selling something that a lot of people buy.

Add complementary products

Selling new products that complement your existing products is called cross-selling. This does not mean that you are going to offer anything that you can think of. If you are selling coffee, selling teaspoons or saucers might work but it is not the perfect complement for coffee. Instead, you can sell creamer, French presses, mugs, and so on. Maybe you can sell teaspoons and saucers but only when you already have these other complementary products.

Again, put yourself in the shoes of your customer. If you buy coffee, what's the next thing that you need to buy? Teaspoons? Of course not. Creamer or sugar, maybe? Definitely. By selling complementary products, you are increasing the checkout price that the customer is going to pay even though he or she was only planning to buy coffee. With that being said, one advantage of cross-selling is increasing your sales because they buy more products from you.

Selling complementary products also improves customer loyalty. This is because your customers will feel satisfied whenever they buy from your shop because they have everything they need. It improves customer experience, which results in loyalty to your brand. Selling complementary products is also easy to manage because it is like buying a bundle. And you know that it is more cost-effective and easier to manage if one person buys two complementary products than if two people buy one same product each. This is also a great way to introduce less popular products. If you really want to sell your teaspoons and saucers, you should first sell your mugs and teacups. This way, people would want to buy the complete set. It would be weird if you're just selling teaspoons and saucers.

There are two terms that you need to know to understand the main objective of cross-selling—skimming and consumer surplus. Skimming is trying to sell a product at the highest price possible at the beginning. Later on, the price of these same products is lowered so that people who are not willing to spend the initial price can also buy the product. Skimming is basically trying to get as much money from your customer as possible. Doesn't sound too ethical, but selling products and starting a business is all about earning profits, right? Not so.

Consumer surplus, on the other hand, is the difference between the amount that a customer is able and willing to pay (depends on the demand) and the amount that they actually spent (depends on the current market price). As the demand for your product decreases, maybe it is no longer trendy or it is almost the end of the season for selling it, the price of your product will decrease. And you can no longer implement skimming because your product is no longer in demand.

Cross-selling helps minimize consumer surplus by offering them a complementary product. Let's say, a customer is willing to spend $50 on a pair of shoes which was trendy months ago, but because of the decrease in demand, you are just selling it for $30, which gives you a $20 consumer surplus. To make the customer spend this amount on your shop, you should try offering complementary products such as socks, insoles, shoelaces, running shorts and t-shirts, and so on. This way, the customer is still spending the entire $50 on your shop. You still make him spend all the money that he is willing and able to spend on your shop.

This is the reason why a lot of businesses bundle things together. Just look at fast food chains like McDonalds, which sells burgers with fries and drinks. Or gaming consoles like Nintendo, which also includes a couple of games and a controller in their bundle. They also upsell by asking you if you want to upsize your drinks and fries or by offering you a higher version of the gaming console.

The key to a successful cross-selling is anticipating your customers' needs. Again, you shouldn't just offer complementary products just for the sake of making an offer because that's just annoying. You need to know if the customer *actually* needs it.

Different ways to cross-sell

a) Sending a follow-up email

You can manually cross-sell by sending an email to your customer. For example, if a customer recently bought a laptop from your shop, you can send a follow up email after a few days offering him accessories such as a laptop bag, mouse, laptop sleeve, and so on.

b) Using a customer's browsing history

There is also automatic cross-selling which Amazon is extremely good at. If a customer visits Amazon and searches for baking sheets, even without actually buying one, your browsing history will be saved. When you visit the website again, you will see suggested products for baking such as baking molds, pans, spatula, rolling pin, and so on.

c) Social proofing

You will also see what other people bought or searched for while you are looking at a particular item. When you see that a lot of people are also buying the same items, you feel more confident about buying the same thing. It's just how humans work. We are social beings, after all, and we value our peer's approval. You will feel that your decision to buy a certain product is validated. Moreover, you will become curious when you see that certain products are bought together by some people. And you will end up buying the bundle yourself because other people are doing it, so there must be a reason.

d) Using a customer's wish list

If you have a wish list saved in your account, they will also customize the suggested products that you see based on the items that you have on your wish list. Your buying history also plays an important role on how the algorithm decides which products you may be interested in.

e) Offering minor yet essential products

You can also sell essential yet minor products to make your main product work. One great example is batteries. If you are selling battery-operated toys, you can be sure that people will also want to buy batteries for these toys. And of course they'd rather buy the batteries from the same store where they bought the toys than to search for them somewhere else. It's not much but it is still a sale.

f) Selling an entire look

Another great example of cross-selling is selling an entire outfit, for those who are selling clothes. You can make suggestions based on what goes well with a particular clothing item. It is just like having a mannequin in your online store. The mannequin gives ideas to potential buyers on how the clothes can be styled and worn. You can do the same thing by creating outfits from your products.

Believe it or not, people who are clueless when it comes to putting together an outfit always appreciate it when there is a complete outfit that they can buy without thinking too much about it. IKEA is also good at this. They showcase room designs using IKEA products and people go crazy over them. They give people ideas on how to decorate their own space using mostly IKEA furniture and décor, of course. This creates a desire among the consumers that they should get the whole look because they can see how great it looks.

When is the best time to cross-sell?

There is not one perfect time to cross-sell because it depends on the customers buying behaviors. However, you might still want to look at the different moments when customers are more willing to buy complementary products.

- You can make offers while the customer is still looking to buy the first product. This is where Amazon comes in. They customize what a buyer can see when they start browsing and shopping by suggesting products that other people bought or products that complement what the customer is planning to buy.

- You can also cross-sell in the shopping cart, just before the customer completes the transaction. This way, they can add the extra before they check out, which will instantly boost your sale for that day.

- There are people who do not want to be distracted during the entire buying process. In this case, it is best to offer them complementary products after completing the transaction, on the thank you page. Some sellers think that the thank you page is not really useful aside from telling the customer that you appreciate their business but it is actually a great page to offer more. They are in a great mood because their transaction was successfully completed and you have their trust and confidence. Plus, they still have their credit card with them so be sure to take advantage of the thank you page.

- You can also send them emails a few days after making a purchase.
- Retargeting, or indirect cross-selling through advertisements, is another great way to offer complementary products. You can use Facebook ads and ads from other platforms to make customers buy complementary products.

You do not have to choose only one method. Just choose which one to use. For instance, if you notice customers are always abandoning their carts, you should not cross-sell before they complete the transaction to prevent distractions. You can also combine two or more methods and test out different strategies at different times to see which ones work best for your business.

Explore opportunities for cross-selling

If you have no idea what to cross-sell, you might want to do a little research for you to get an idea what other products will complement the ones that you are already selling.

- The first thing to do is to check your competitors' listings and see what kind of complementary products they are offering. If you are selling shoes, check out other vendors that sell shoes and see what they offer as add-ons.
- You can also conduct a survey by sending it to your email list or by posting it in your Facebook group. Ask them what they would like to see in your store or what kinds of products would go well with your main products.
- Asking your manufacturer what complementary products they can make is also a great idea. Some people often overlook this step because they think it's all about the customers (it really is most of the time) but you should also look at the kinds of products that your manufacturer makes. This is even more helpful if they are also making products for other Amazon sellers.

Chapter 9

Scaling $10,000 a Month and Beyond

This chapter is the culmination of everything that you have learned in this e-book. Every vendor's end goal is to earn as much income as possible by selling via Amazon FBA. If you just want to help people, maybe you should just donate to charity? This is real life and in real life, you need money to pay the bills and take care of your family & loved ones. And you can earn good money by selling on Amazon. It would be even better if you can earn at least $10,000 or even more by selling on Amazon.

This is achievable because a lot of people are earning five to six figures on Amazon. How can you do that? Here are some of the important steps that have been discussed in the previous chapters and additional information that can turn your business into a money-making machine.

1. Continue evolving as a business

Coca-Cola and Apple did not reach this level of success because they have remained the same. Times change and the needs of the people and their buying behavior change as well. If your business cannot keep up with the changing times, you will surely be left behind.

A lot of people change their branding to make them look more modern. One popular example is the logo of Lord and Taylor or Instagram. They used to have logos that look old school and traditional but they changed them to make them more suitable for the modern consumers.

Another thing that you should do is to add new products, improve existing products, and add complementary products. You already know that doing these things can only lead to a significant increase in sales. Cross-selling was discussed in depth in the previous chapter, and how selling one product can lead to sales of another related product. This is why selling complementary products can improve your business.

However, keep in mind that it is best to approach this method slowly because adding too many products at the onset can be detrimental to your business. Startups should not use all their money buying different kinds of stuff to sell. It is hard to take action if your money is tied up to your inventory. It is also harder to keep track of the items that sell and the items that don't because you have way too many to track. It is also more difficult to build a core community because your customers have different interests. You can release more products once you know how your initial products did in the market.

Aside from changing your branding and adding and changing products, you should also consider adding value to your brand. For example, consumers these days are more conscious about buying things. A lot of people prefer sustainable brands which are generally lesser known than mainstream brands. This is because they promote sustainability, they are cruelty-free, they are ethical, and they are vegan. They are sometimes even more expensive than mainstream brands, but people still buy them because of this advocacy. You should also consider doing this to your brand. Make it sustainable, if you can. However, you shouldn't just do it for the sake of earning more profits. You need to do it for the right reasons for it to be successful.

2. Build an online community

These days, it is important to have an online community of people who love your products. You should never underestimate the power of social media in terms of influencing others to make decisions. These online communities such as Facebook groups and fan pages can be great support hubs for people who need help with your products. They serve as a place for updating and educating others about your business. If a new customer has a question about the product that he just bought, the community can help him by sharing their own experiences or information that they gathered from other resources. One perfect example is Amazon's Seller Central where you can discuss certain topics and issues with other sellers.

The fact that there is a community of people that joined together because of your product says a lot about your business. It means that a lot of people patronize your business and love your products, and are willing to meet others who share the same interests. These loyal customers will keep buying from you. This is why you should take care of them and make them feel appreciated. Maybe you can conduct raffles and contests for those people who are a part of your online community. Maybe you can give promo codes to those who are members of your Facebook group. Do these things and they will love you even more.

3. Continue doing product launches

If you think a product launch is only done at the start of your business, you are wrong because you can continue doing product launches as long as you have new or improved products to sell. This is why your products have to keep on evolving. You already know that doing product launches can lead to a high volume of traffic that can then be converted to sales. If you have product launches every time you have a new product or an improved feature of an existing product, just imagine how much income you will earn.

Just like what you did in your very first launch, you should also send out emails to your email list and invite people in your Facebook community to participate. The difference between your very first launch and your subsequent launches is that you now have more people in your email list and in your community. You already have loyal customers. Before, everyone was new to your product and they didn't know much about your business. You may have had achieved high traffic during your product launch, but a lot of them probably didn't end up buying. This will change when you do your succeeding launches because you now have a bigger following who know about your product and your business.

Releasing teasers leading up to the launch can also build up the hype and interest in your new product. You can maybe post a riddle about your new product days in advance. You can also conduct a countdown. Doing things like this will make the launch more exciting, and people will surely anticipate what you have in store for them. Just make sure that your product will live up to the expectation of your customers, especially since you are responsible for building up the excitement over your product.

4. Continue optimizing your product listing

Optimizing your product listing is something that you should not overlook because how your customers see your product can make or break a sale. Your product listing is the first thing that Amazon users see when they search for certain keywords in the search field. It is important that they find your listing easy to understand by presenting all the important details and information about the product as straightforwardly as possible.

If they are satisfied with the image and description, and they think that your product is what they are looking for, they will surely buy it and who knows? Maybe they will come back and buy more next time. To ensure that your product is presented as accurately as possible and that it is visible whenever an Amazon user searched for that kind of product, you need to optimize your product listing. It increases traffic to your shop, boosts sales conversion, and therefore improves profits.

The anatomy of a highly profitable product listing consists of a title, images, key product features, description, product reviews, and rating. The first four parts are the seller's responsibility and the last two come from the customers. It is not their responsibility to write a review or leave a rating, which is why you need to encourage them to do so. This will be discussed next.

5. Increase social proof

Social proof is a psychological phenomenon wherein people are more likely to do certain actions because other people are doing it as well. Knowing that someone else has already bought the product and is using it will make a consumer more confident and at ease in buying the same product for the first time. It's like people are looking for validation for their actions. In fact, study shows that product reviews are 12 times more trusted than the product description itself. You want to hear what people who have used the product have to say.

You always witness and experience social proof in your day to day life. You are more likely to eat in a restaurant filled with diners than an empty one. You have seen online clothing stores posting pictures of celebrities wearing the same clothes they are selling. People line up to buy milk tea, the latest iPhone, and so on. You think these products are worth your money because others are also buying them. Social proof is everywhere and you can also use this to your advantage.

The most important social proofing technique that you can do is to gather reviews from your customers. You can send follow up emails to customers asking them to write a review and rate the product. You can also ask your most loyal customers to create a video testimonial and post it on Amazon. Products that have more reviews are more likely to attract buyers because of social proof.

Your target should be to get 4 to 5 stars. If you have mostly 4 or 5 stars, you are on the right track. If not, you should understand why people are giving you a rating lower than 4. You need to read your bad reviews as well and do something about it. Maybe it is something that can be fixed. And gathering as much positive reviews and rating as you can will balance out a few negative reviews. As long as you only have a couple of negative reviews, you will be fine. Potential buyers will just think that the customer who gave you a bad review is difficult to please if the rest gave you positive reviews.

6. Gain more visibility using AMS

Amazon Marketing Services or AMS can help improve your product rank and your listing gain more visibility. As discussed earlier, AMS is a tool used by sellers to run ads. The ads are pay-per-click, which means that you only have to pay when an Amazon user clicks the ad. This is a great way to make your listings more visible. It is easy to set up AMS. Just login to your Amazon advertising console account and just follow the steps. When customers see your products all the time, you can be sure that your income will increase dramatically.

7. Explore creating a YouTube channel

If you want to maximize all the social media platforms, you should not forget YouTube. YouTube is a great platform for influencers and sellers because they attract huge traffic to their online stores like Amazon. For instance, a lot of resellers on online selling platforms such as eBay, Poshmark, and Depop have YouTube accounts and have hundreds of thousands of subscribers and viewers. These people may not know about their online store but after watching their YouTube videos, they will visit the store and end up buying what they have seen in the video.

Creating a YouTube channel does not only drive traffic to your online store. It can also be another source of income in itself. It is definitely a win-win situation for you because not only are you boosting your Amazon sales, you are also earning money from your YouTube videos. For instance, if you are selling clothes on Amazon, you can do a haul or a look book video using all your products for sale. People who love watching YouTube videos may see your video and love one particular outfit. They may not have bought anything from Amazon before, but they might just start now after seeing your video. If you are selling software, you can create YouTube tutorial videos. You do not really need to be in front of the camera if you are a shy person. You can ask someone to model the clothes for you or you can just simply do a voiceover and just record your tutorial on your computer.

These are the things that you can do to earn $10,000 or even more via Amazon FBA. It is definitely hard work, but everything is worth it once you start seeing the money rolling in.

Conclusion

I'd like to congratulate you for completing this book from start to finish.

I hope this book was able to help you to learn everything you need to know about selling via Amazon FBA.

The next step is to take action and do everything you have learned in this book. Come up with a product that you can sell if you haven't thought of anything yet or contact a manufacturer.

I wish you the best of luck!

Please Review This Book

A lot of effort went into writing this book to appeal to loyal readers like YOU. Please, I'd appreciate if you can spare a few seconds of your time to leave a review and let me know your thoughts! Thanks a LOT.

Introduction

The internet has opened a lot of doors for aspiring online entrepreneurs. Anyone with an idea and the resolve to pursue such an idea can start and build a successful online business. It so happens that one of the most lucrative business ideas today is dropshipping. Dropshipping is popular for the simple reason that it follows a business model which is perfect for the digital age. There are numerous definitions for dropshipping that are being thrown out there. But in the simplest of terms, it's a type of business that follows the traditional buy-and-sell model. Only this time, you don't need to get your hands on the inventory. You simply act as the middleman between the product manufacturer or supplier and the consumer.

The business model looks simple on paper. However, without the right information, it can be difficult to execute. This is why I have decided to write this book to help you fully understand how dropshipping works and how you can create your own successful dropshipping business. There are so many factors involved in setting up a dropshipping business. I will be discussing every single one of these factors in this book.

Be that as it may, I need to emphasize here that this book is not a blueprint for some get-rich-quick scheme. If you are looking for a get-rich-quick business model, then this book is not for you. You don't get instantly rich after starting a Dropshipping business. Sure, there are some who get lucky and earn a ton of money from the get-go. But these are few and far in between. Moreover, building a sustainable business requires the right knowledge, mindset and perseverance - not luck. This is why before you continue reading this book, I need you to have *realistic expectations*. Just like any form of business, dropshipping requires time and efforts to be profitable. It can take weeks or months before you see any meaningful profits going your way. That's the reality.

I'm not saying this to discourage you or downplay the merits of dropshipping. I'm telling you this to make sure that you get started with the right mindset, realistic goals and actionable plans. **These are the keys to achieving success in dropshipping.** You have to come up with goals that are achievable based on your current knowledge, skillset, and experience. To reach these goals, you also need a comprehensive plan which describes in detail the steps that you are going to take. If you have these, then you are off to a good start. You have a good foundation that will be of great help to you in the long run.

A very common question among beginners in the dropshipping industry is this: "Is the business model sustainable?" My answer is yes, it is indeed sustainable. However, you shouldn't confuse the term sustainable with the term profitable. Just because a business model is sustainable doesn't necessarily mean it's profitable. You have to always keep that in mind. Building a sustainable and profitable dropshipping business requires the *right knowledge*, time and effort. There are no shortcuts to success here. You have to focus on improving and building the business day in and day out.

I want this book to serve as your guide as you navigate through the complicated world of dropshipping. Whether you are a complete beginner or someone who has some experience in the industry, there's a ton of information in this book that you are going to find valuable. Even after finishing this book, you can always use it as a reference for questions and problems you might encounter in the future. With that said, I suggest that you always keep a copy of this book in your files for easy access and reference.

How much you earn from your dropshipping business depends on a lot of factors. But I'm here to tell you right now that it's possible to make five figures each month from your business. Thousands of other people are doing it. So why can't you? Yes, you can reach $10,000 a month or even go beyond that amount with the right products coupled with a great marketing strategy. The icing on the cake is the possibility that you can earn this amount on autopilot. That is not an exaggeration. You definitely can earn thousands of dollars a month through dropshipping after setting things up the right way. That is the beauty of dropshipping. You can automate most of the processes involved in the business.

Before you dig into this book, there's one last tip I want to tell you. Don't rush! This is something I always tell people who wish to start their own dropshipping business. Majority of those who rush their businesses skip a couple of crucial steps and eventually fail. Don't make the same mistake. What you need to do is build your business one day at a time. Make a detailed plan for everything that you want to accomplish. Before you make any decision, make sure that it's backed up by good data and information. Don't make decisions on instincts alone. Relying solely on our instincts is risky and a common cause of failure.

Without further ado, lets get right into it!

Did You Know

71% of shoppers believe they will get a better deal online than in stores.
Are you aware of what campaigns your competitors are running both in-store and online?

Chapter 1

Understanding Dropshipping

Dropshipping is not exactly a brand new concept. The business model has been around for decades even before the arrival of the internet. Some enterprising people would put up ads in local newspapers, in the radio, or on television informing consumers that they are selling this or that product. But they don't actually own or have these products on hand. If a customer calls to buy a product, what these entrepreneurs do is get in touch with a supplier or a manufacturer, buy the product, and instruct the supplier to ship the product directly to the customer. The entrepreneurs make money on the difference between the product's advertised price and the supplier's price.

This is basically the precursor to today's version of dropshipping. The internet has completely revolutionized the business model. It made it very easy to move products from anywhere in the world. All you need to do is set up a website, install a piece of dropshipping software, and you are good to go. You can literally do everything from the comfort of your home. You don't hold any inventory. You don't do the shipping. Your responsibilities only involve running the website and making deals with suppliers and manufacturers.

The online dropshipping model rode on the back of online retail sites. When the internet first came about, most people used it merely for research and entertainment. Then businesses and enterprising individuals saw the internet's potential as a marketplace for products and services. Ecommerce quickly boomed and grew at a very fast pace. Businesses would build websites and sell their products and services there. For a while, ecommerce only had people and businesses selling their own products and services. But there soon came a shift when ecommerce concepts like affiliate marketing were introduced. People who don't have their own products and services now have the chance to make money through ecommerce.

In a way, online dropshipping is an offshoot of affiliate marketing. You are basically promoting and selling someone else's products. However, in the dropshipping model, you have the option of rebranding the products as if they are your own. You can make a deal with a supplier or manufacturer who produces the products then marks them with your customized labels. You purchase the products at cost basis (i.e. original cost) then resell them with a marked up price (i.e. original cost + your profit). In short, as a dropshipper, you are not a product developer or manufacturer. You are merely a marketer.

As I've mentioned earlier, online dropshipping has revolutionized online commerce. And it continues to evolve as we speak. In fact, dropshipping has become so big that it can be aptly considered as an industry on its own. Online dropshipping registers billions of sales a year. This will only grow in the coming years as more and more people get involved in the business. Almost every product today can be sold using the dropshipping model. You just have to find and approach the right suppliers and manufacturers.

It also does not matter where you are located. As long as you have a reliable internet connection, you can build and run an online dropshipping operation. You can be in Antarctica and still run a successful dropshipping business that ships products from China to the United States. Or you could be vacationing in Thailand and still run a business that dropships products from Brazil to Australia. My point here is that this business model offers time and location freedom. You can run your business from anywhere and at any time.

Another good reason why now is the time to be involved in dropshipping is the availability of tools and resources that make the process so much easier. In the early days, online entrepreneurs had to build everything from scratch. This meant that you had to be a programmer or you needed to hire a team of programmers to help you set up your website. Today, you can build a fully-functioning dropshipping website in minutes by just clicking on a few buttons and following step-by-step, beginner friendly instructions. There are all sorts of software that you can download and install on your dropshipping website. Some of these software programs automate your website so that you don't have to do anything else. The website will run itself with you doing very minimal work. This is one of the reasons why this business model was awarded a simplicity and passivity score of 80% in the book <u>Passive Income Ideas: 50 Ways To Make Money Online Analyzed.</u>

Before we proceed to the next chapter, let's make sure that you fully understand how online dropshipping works. Basically, here are the main steps involved in dropshipping:
- **Step 1**: You build a website that's specifically designed for dropshipping.
- **Step 2**: You get into a deal with a supplier or manufacturer to produce the products you are going to sell.
- **Step 3**: Promote the products on your website.
- **Step 4**: If someone orders a product from your website, you order the product from your supplier or manufacturer.
- **Step 5**: Your supplier is automatically informed about the order.
- **Step 6**: Your supplier or manufacturer ships the product to the buyer.
- **Step 7**: Rinse and repeat.

Chapter Summary

The business model for online dropshipping is pretty straightforward. You build the website, make a deal with a supplier, promote the product, and instruct the supplier to ship the product directly to customers. It's basically buying and reselling products but this time, you don't hold any inventory. You simply do the marketing and selling. Your supplier handles product development, manufacturing, and shipping. It's a business model that is perfect suited to today's digitally connected world. The barriers to setting up a dropshipping business are very minimal. Remember that you are not going to hold inventory. This zero inventory benefit drives down your startup costs. In a nutshell, all you need to get started is a deal with a supplier or manufacturer, a functioning dropshipping website, and a reliable internet connection.

Did You Know

70% of E-Commerce traffic is from smartphones. Is your website and your products being represented on a retailer's website optimised for mobile? Watch out for truncated product descriptions.

Other Notable Books By Michael Ezeanaka	
Book #	**Book Title**
1	Affiliate Marketing Made Easy
2	55 Passive Income Ideas Analysed
3	Amazon FBA Mastery
4	Dropshipping
5	Real Estate Investing For Beginners
6	Credit Card Mastery
7	Facebook Advertising Made Easy
8	Stock Market Investing For Beginners
The kindle edition will be available to you for FREE when you purchase the paperback version from Amazon.com (The US Store)	

Chapter 2

Benefits Of The Dropshipping Model

Why would you build a dropshipping business instead of other alternative online business models? This is a very important question which we will address in this chapter. One of the reasons why some people tend to downplay the merits of dropshipping is that they aren't fully aware of the benefits that it offers. On paper or through the definition alone, dropshipping seems like a simple business that can only earn you spare change. That isn't the case at all. As I've said in the Introduction, you can earn as much as $10,000 a month from dropshipping if you do it right.

Anyway, let us go back to the question. Why would you spend your time and efforts in building an online dropshipping business? Well, lets see.

1. Dropshipping Requires Very Little Capital Investment

This is without a doubt the most important benefit of starting a dropshipping business. Dropshipping won't cost you an arm and a leg. Always keep in mind that in dropshipping, you are not holding any inventory. Unlike a traditional business model wherein you buy products then resell them, dropshipping involves purchasing the product only when a customer makes an order. You only make some sort of expense when a customer buys from you. But that expense basically means nothing because you are turning a profit from every sale you make.

The costs associated with starting a dropshipping business are mostly related to setting up the dropshipping website; like web development costs, web hosting costs, domain registration costs, and other technical expenses related to creating and maintaining the website. You also have to spend money in order to drive traffic to your website via Google ads, Facebook ads, Instagram etc.

Furthermore, you may also have to pay for the tools, software programs, plugins, and add-ons that you are going to use in your dropshipping website. Some of these are one-time costs. Others are recurring costs (i.e. plugins that require you to pay a monthly subscription fee).

As far as inventory costs are concerned, your expenses will depend on the negotiations and deals that you enter into with your supplier or manufacturer. For sure, there will be inventory costs especially if you are going to customize or rebrand a product and sell it as if you've made it yourself. With this practice, you will have to have a sample batch developed and manufactured. Needless to say, this isn't going to be free. You have to pay for the sample batch of products. Even with these expenses, they are still very minimal compared to the costs you would have incurred if you follow a traditional buy-and-sell business model.

My main point here is that no matter what angle you look at it, dropshipping requires relatively little capital investment from you. Your finances are easily manageable right from the start. With just a few hundred dollars, you can start a fully-functioning dropshipping website and business. With that said, there aren't much financial barriers when it comes to starting and building an online dropshipping business.

2. It's Super Easy to Get Started

Would you believe me if I tell you that you can get a dropshipping business fully running within an hour? It's probably hard to believe, but it's definitely possible. That's how easy it is to get started with dropshipping. I have mentioned earlier the availability of tools, plugins, and pieces of software that are *specifically designed for dropshipping processes*. These tools make it hassle-free to start and run a dropshipping business. These can also be used to automate the business so you don't have to do everything on your own.

You don't need much to launch a dropshipping business. A website and the product, these are the two most important things you need. Getting the website isn't difficult. There are tons of pre-made templates out there for dropshipping websites. Feel free to check out the options available at ThemeForest, Shopify and plenty other vendors out there. Just get one of these templates, customize it depending on your specific needs and preferences, and upload the products you are promoting and selling. If you have programming or coding skills, doing these should be a breeze. If you are not that technically proficient, you can always outsource the responsibilities to a freelancer or contractor. Freelancers can be hired from sites like upwork, fiverr etc.

When getting started, my advice for you is that you decide first on the types of products you are going to promote before you begin building the website. The reason why you should follow this strategy is that it's easier to build a website if you know the products that you are going to sell. You will know which features you need and what kind of content you are going to publish on the site. If you are outsourcing the website-building process, the web developer will have an idea of the direction you want to take.

3. There's Less Overhead Costs

For a lot of traditional online businesses, overhead costs are a huge problem. You don't have this problem if you are running a dropshipping operation. Since you are not keeping any inventory of the products you are selling, and let's keep in mind that overhead costs are usually related to inventory management, you don't have inventory so there's nothing to manage. That's a significant chunk of overhead costs that you take off your plate. These include:

- **Cost of space** - facility in which the inventory is housed i.e. warehouse depreciation, insurance, utilities, warehouse staff, storage racks etc.
- **Cost of money** - Interest cost associated with the cost of borrowing money to pay for inventory e.g. bank loans, credit cards etc.
- **Cost of obsolescence** - Some inventory item may never be used or will be damaged while in storage, and so must be disposed of at a reduced price, or at no price at all. Depending on how perishable the inventory is, or the speed with which technology changes impact inventory values, this can be a substantial cost.

Another great thing about the dropshipping model is that your overhead costs usually go down as time goes by. A huge portion of your overhead costs are spent on your first weeks and months. As you build your business, these overhead costs normally decrease with time. Why is this the case? In the first stages of your business, you are basically still learning the ropes so you are prone to risks and mistakes. These risks and mistakes often result to overhead expenses. But as you refine your business and find more efficient ways to run things, these risks and mistakes eventually go away. Fewer risks and fewer mistakes mean you will have less overhead expenses.

4. Access to a Wide Selection of Products

If a product can be shipped whether domestically or internationally, you can market and sell it via dropshipping. There are literally hundreds of thousands of products out there that you can sell through the dropshipping model. All you have to do is choose. A common misconception about dropshipping is that you can only sell one or two products through a dropshipping website. This is not true. You can sell dozens or even hundreds of products in your online store and dropship every single one of them. For sure, as you add more products to your selection, the harder it gets to manage the varying orders. But that's not the point. The point here is that there is no ceiling to the number of unique products that you can promote and sell through a dropshipping website.

However, if it's your first time starting a dropshipping business, I would recommend that you start with just one or two products. You are new so you are still learning the ropes. With a few products in your plate, it's going to be much easier to run and manage the business. As you gain more experience, you can then start introducing additional products into the mix. The lesson here is that you shouldn't bite more than what you can chew.

5. It's Not That Difficult to Scale

With the dropshipping model, all you need to do to scale your business is add more products to your selection or you start another dropshipping website that offers a new selection of products. Setting up another website will only require a small amount of time and efforts from you especially if you are utilizing a ready-made template. With a dropshipping template, all you have to do is customize the look of the website, upload your product images and descriptions, add information about your business, and install any needed plugins or software programs.

It's definitely possible for you to start and run several dropshipping businesses at the same time. As I have said in an earlier chapter, there's nothing to stop you from starting as many dropshipping websites as you can. If you can manage and run all of them, then by all means, go for it. I know of some online entrepreneurs who manage dozens of dropshipping websites so it can definitely be done. This is why you should learn everything you can about online business automation. You have to take advantage of all the tools and resources that allow you to automate your business processes.

And just so you know, this was one of the most scalable businesses analyzed in the book <u>Passive Income Ideas: 50 Ways to Make Money Online Analyzed,</u> with a scalability score of 90%!

6. Access to a Global Market

With the dropshipping model, you can promote and sell products to anyone in the world provided that your supplier or manufacturer has the means to ship the products there. That is the beauty of online commerce. With just a simple website, you have the ability to reach out to millions of potential customers. However, before you offer global shipping, make sure that you are fully aware of the associated costs. You have to look into the costs of shipping a product to every country. These costs often vary so you need to be careful.

I personally know of a few dropshippers who made the mistake of not learning about shipping costs per country before offering global shipping for their customers. They ended up losing a lot of money because of this simple mistake. You have to understand that shipping costs per country are always different. For example, let's say that your supplier ships products from China. The cost of shipping a product from China to the United States is different to the cost of shipping the same product to Brazil.

So how do you solve this glaring problem? What most dropshipping entrepreneurs do is **price their products based on the geographical location of the buyer**. A person from Brazil sees a different price point compared to a person from the United States. For example, the price for United States customers may be $15 while the price for Brazil customers is $10. The price all depends on the shipping costs associated with that country. If the shipping cost is higher, the price of the product will reasonably be higher as well.

For this to work, you need to **build a dynamic website** wherein a visitor from the United States sees $15 while a visitor from Brazil sees $10. It's all about catering to the customer based on where he or she is located. This enables you to offer your product to a global market. A tool that can potentially help with this is an app called <u>Multi Country Pricing</u>. As of writing, it's currently available in the Shopify app store. There could be plenty other resources like this to assist you!

7. It Can Be Easily Automated

Advances in online commerce have made it very easy to get things done. With just a few clicks of the mouse button, you are able to build a fully-functioning website. With just a simple plugin, the customer service feature on your website can be managed by a chatbot that runs on artificial intelligence (AI). By installing a piece of software, anyone can order and pay for products on your website. These are just some of the instances where you can see automation in action. All of these are applicable in the dropshipping industry.

Automation allows the business to run and manage itself with very minimal intervention from you. This is every online entrepreneur's dream. The business runs itself and continues to process orders and sales even when you are sleeping or if you are vacationing in the Virgin Islands. As long as there are no bugs or errors in the system, you continue making money. In short, dropshipping is one of the few businesses that can help you earn a consistent stream of passive income. You keep on earning money with very little work. You don't even have to keep inventories of your products. You don't even ship the products. All you do is drive customers to your website, accept the orders, process them, and forward them to your supplier or manufacturer who handles the rest of the transaction cycle.

8. There's No Shortage of Suppliers and Manufacturers

Do something for me, will you? Go to Google and search for Alibaba. Visit the website and browse there for a bit and get an understanding of what the website is and what it does. Are you done? It's an immense marketplace, is it not? Almost every product you can conceive of is available there for sale and for bulk purchase. Hundreds of thousands of merchants, traders, suppliers, and manufacturers strut their wares on the site. This is why Alibaba is one of the biggest sources of dropshipped products in the world today. This is not an exaggeration. You have access to very cheap products that you can customize, rebrand, and resell at premium prices.

And here's the thing. Alibaba is just the tip of the iceberg. It's just one of dozens of online marketplaces where you can find products to promote and dropship in your own store. Alibaba is based in China and it's by far the go-to marketplace for a lot of dropshippers. What makes Alibaba so popular among dropshippers is that the marketplace offers the cheapest prices in the industry. If for some reason you can't do business with Alibaba, worry not, because you have a lot of other options. You just have to look for them. It all depends on the types of products that you plan on dropshipping.

Chapter Summary

The bottom line here is that dropshipping is an ultimately viable business opportunity which offers a lot of benefits to both aspiring and established online entrepreneurs. The barriers to entry are very minimal so anyone can start a dropshipping business. You don't need a thick wallet to get started. In a lot of cases, just a few hundred dollars will do. Furthermore, there is no ceiling to how much you can scale the business. You can start a dozen dropshipping sites if you want to as long as you have the time and the manpower to run all of them. In a nutshell, the dropshipping model offers a variety of benefits that make it very appealing to those looking to make money online.

Did You Know

38% cite social media interaction as their reason for visiting a retailers website. Does your brand have a strong social media strategy to drive traffic?

Chapter 3

Disadvantages of The Dropshipping Model

Since we have discussed the benefits and rewards of engaging in a dropshipping business, it's important that we also discuss its possible drawbacks. I will be the first to tell you that the dropshipping model is not a perfect business model. Just like any business opportunity, it has its own flaws. And that's what we are going to discuss in this chapter. That being said, these drawbacks should not in any way discourage you. I'm telling you these so that you will know what to expect and what kinds of risks you will be facing when you finally embark in your dropshipping journey. This way, you'll be able to make an informed decision.

1. Sudden Stock Shortages

This is one of the most common problems with the dropshipping model. There are always huge ups and downs with the way product orders are made. Let's say for instance that in one given week, you receive a few orders a day. What if in the next week, orders suddenly balloon to hundreds of orders a day? In most of these scenarios, the supplier or manufacturer won't be able to fulfill the orders as fast as you would want them to. Stock availability is really something that you don't have complete control over. This can be very problematic if there's no consistency in the way customers order products from your dropshipping website. That being said, this problem can be managed by using Google Trends website to monitor the seasonality of a product, anticipate periods of large demands e.g. during festive periods and having multiple suppliers capable of matching the demand.

2. Higher Cost of Goods Sold

The cost of goods sold is higher in the sense that you pay more for the goods if you are a dropshipper compared to the price being paid by a stocking retailer. A stocking retailer is someone who buys the products before reselling them (i.e. direct retailers, supermarkets, grocery stores). It's understandable why suppliers and manufacturers offer lower prices to these stocking retailers. This is something you must take seriously especially if you are going to dropship products that are already available in supermarkets and other retail outlets. Since your cost of goods sold are higher, your prices will often be higher compared to other retailers.

3. Higher Fulfillment Costs

Here's something you need to understand about the dropshipping process. You are not only paying for the cost of the goods. You are also paying for the costs associated with stocking, picking, packing, packaging, and shipping. This means you are dealing with a huge mark-up. Of course, you can cut down the costs by negotiating with your supplier and manufacturer but the fulfilment costs will still be high.

4. More Customer Service Issues

The shipping aspect of the business may be under the control of your supplier but customer service is still your responsibility. It's not that difficult to see why this can cause a lot of headaches to you. You are not the one handling the packaging and shipping duties so you are often clueless how and when the products get to your customers. This is a recipe for disaster as far as customer service is concerned. There are so many factors that you have to know about the shipping process in order to be able to provide answers and solutions to disgruntled customers. You have to know when the product was shipped, what the tracking details are, and the estimated arrival time of the product. To know these things, you have to be communicating with your supplier and manufacturer.

5. You Don't Have Full Control Over the Business

This is a no-brainer but a lot of aspiring dropshippers tend to ignore it until it hits them in the head. Letting a separate entity take charge of your product handling and shipping process is very risky, to say the least. It's great if your supplier or manufacturer does a great job. But what if it keeps delaying its shipments or if it doesn't ship the products the right way such that a lot of the products get damaged or even lost along the way? You know that when this happens, the customers will be blaming you, not the supplier. Your brand (if any) will suffer the consequences. This is why I always advise aspiring dropshippers to make sure that a supplier is trustworthy and reliable before making a deal with him/her.

6. Reliance on Stocks

This is very similar to stock shortages. You are relying on the good faith of the supplier that the stocks will always be available. Let's be honest here. 100% of your business relies on the stocks being held by your supplier. If you get orders from customers and your supplier tells you that stocks aren't available for now, that's not good. If this happens too often, you might as well close your shop. So I need to repeat my advice above. Only enter into deals with suppliers and manufacturers who have proven themselves to be reliable. Your business literally stands on their reliability. To avoid being over reliant on one supplier build relationships with multiple suppliers.

7. Potential Quality Control Issues

Again, you are not developing, manufacturing, and handling the products you are selling. In short, you have very little control on the products including their quality. Quality control is one of the things that you have to sacrifice if you engage in a dropshipping business. You can try to agree on quality issues with the supplier but this doesn't always mean that the quality standards will remain the same. You just have to hope that the supplier delivers his other end of the deal. Since you don't hold any of the inventory, you will only hear about a decrease in product quality if you start receiving an uptick in customer complaints and product returns. By this time, the damage has already been done. You have to rebuild once again a positive relationship between you and your customers. In a nutshell, if you plan on starting a dropshipping business, keep in mind that product quality is something that you have very minimal control over.

8. Overcrowded Markets

In many ways, dropshipping has gone mainstream and the competition among sellers is growing tougher by the day. A lot of the markets being targeted by dropshippers are overcrowded already. It's easy to set up a dropshipping store so anyone who knows how online commerce works can start his own dropshipping operation. The competition will only get worse in the coming months and years as more and more people attempt to get a piece of the action. I guess what I'm trying to say here is that you have to be ready to compete with hundreds or even thousands of other sellers when you set up your own dropshipping business. You can minimize this by conducting good product research and niching down to product categories that have good demand but not as much competition. Later in this book, you'll discover how to go about doing that.

9. No Guarantee of Profits

There is this common misconception that it's easy to be profitable in dropshipping because you don't hold any inventory. People often assume that you are reaping huge rewards from every sale because you didn't have anything to do with the production and shipping of the products. But just like any business, there's no guarantee of profits here. There are various factors that can cause things to go wrong. You might suddenly lose the deal with your supplier. Your manufacturer might produce a product that's subpar. You may have overestimated your potential market. Or the products just don't sell. Any of these problems can occur. Not only won't you be profitable, you will likely lose some money as well. In other words, don't expect dropshipping to be a 100% guaranteed easy route to business profitability. There is no such thing.

10. Requires *Basic* Technical Skills

In a lot of ways, online dropshipping is a very technical business. Always remember that many aspects of the business involves building and managing a website. This means you should at least have *basic* knowledge of web development and coding or access to freelancers with the knowledge. This is especially important if you are running the business on your own. You must have the technical knowledge and skills to keep the website running smoothly without major glitches.

You should also have the capability to fix technical problems. What if the website suddenly goes down? What if a customer can't place an order? What if the customer's payment is not going through? What if the website takes forever to load? These are just a few of the potential problems that your website might encounter. It's important that you have what it takes to fix them as soon as possible. If you are not confident with your technical skills, then you should hire someone who is. Dropshipping requires a lot of technical work. There's no other way around this. Either you do the technical work yourself or you get a skilled and experienced professional to do it for you.

11. More Products or More Suppliers Means More Work

Scaling a dropshipping business is very doable but you have to be aware that if you double your list of products, you are also doubling the amount of work that you have to do. This is why many online dropshippers are often not that enthusiastic to add more products to their listings because they are adding more work upon themselves. It gets even more complicated if you are working with more than one supplier. There may be instances wherein one product comes from one supplier and another product comes from a different supplier. Tracking and managing different products and different suppliers can be challenging.

My advice for you is that you shouldn't bite off more than you can chew. Start with a single product. If you can easily manage the work it demands, then you should probably add another product in your listings. If you can manage the two products, then you can add a third product. My main point here is that you add products to your business in a slow and gradual way. Don't add too many products at the same time. Doing so might overwhelm you. Your best strategy is to add the products one at a time.

Be that as it may, much of this task can be outsourced to freelancers who will help you handle customer service and other menial tasks associated with this business.

12. Low Margins

This often flies under the radar when it comes to newbies starting a dropshipping business. A lot of beginners tend to assume that dropshipping always comes with high profit margins. Again, this is mostly because of the fact that they neither handle nor keep the products. This often makes beginners think that they will be dealing with very low product costs. That's not the case at all. As I've mentioned earlier, it's actually more expensive to dropship a product than purchase them in bulk and sell them as a direct retailer.

Since you are buying the products at higher costs as a dropshipper, this means that you will be left with lower profit margins. This will always be the case if the dropshipping model doesn't go through major changes. Another thing you should always remember is that you are not just competing with other sellers online, you are also competing with offline sellers. You have to put a price tag on your products that's reasonable in the context of both your online and offline competition.

13. Inventory Issues

There are a lot of things that can go wrong with the products you are selling. The problem is that you usually don't have any control of these issues. If something goes wrong with the inventory, it's usually the fault of the supplier or manufacturer. But the problem will still be reflected upon your business. Your customers will be looking at you for answers. Keep in mind that your customers don't know that you are the middleman. They think that you make and ship the products yourself. With that said, every problem they see in the products will be blamed upon you.

Problems with inventories are without a doubt one of the biggest drawbacks of online dropshipping. Making matters worse is the fact that these problems are often way beyond your control. The most effective way of avoiding these problems is to only deal with suppliers and manufacturers who are reliable. You should be able to trust them. They should have a good track record. Always check their backgrounds and their ratings before you enter into any deals with them. Most online marketplaces these days have rating systems for suppliers and manufacturers. If a supplier has **been around for a long time and has a lot of good ratings** from entrepreneurs they've worked with in the past, then that supplier is most likely a good bet. If it's the other way around, then you are better off looking for another supplier.

14. Shipping Complexities

Shipping a product to a customer is never an easy task. The good news is that this responsibility lies not in you but in your supplier or manufacturer. However, this doesn't mean that you can ignore the complexity of the process. There must be a smooth connection between your sales process and the supplier's shipping procedures. In this way, when a customer orders a product from your dropshipping website, your supplier is immediately informed about the order. The faster the supplier is informed about the sale, the quicker he will be able to ship the product to the customer. If there isn't an efficient communication line between your business website and the supplier, this is where shipping complexities arise and cause havoc to the business.

15. Supplier Errors

Your supplier or manufacturer will be making errors. This is something you have to take into account. No supplier or manufacturer is perfect. They all have their flaws and they are not immune to making errors. A supplier error can be anything. It could be the wrong product being sent to the customer. It could be the right product but it was sent to the wrong customer. Products with the wrong specifications being sent to customers are a common occurrence in the dropshipping industry. It happens all the time and it can be very frustrating because as a dropshipper, you don't have control over these errors. If a customer complains about receiving the wrong product, then you have to work to ensure that the product is recalled and that the right product is resent.

Chapter Summary

As you can see, the dropshipping business model has a lot of inherent flaws. There are so many things that can go wrong. **Being aware of these potential problems can help prepare you in dealing with them.** The gist of this chapter is that dropshipping isn't a perfect business model. It's easy to get into the business but it can be complicated if you're not adequately prepared. What's frustrating is that a lot of these problems are often not under your control. They are usually not your fault, to put it simply. However, don't let these drawbacks discourage you from starting and building an online dropshipping business. Let these drawbacks serve as reminders why you need to be smarter and more careful in running your business. Also, knowing about these drawbacks enable you to come up with solutions when you encounter any of the problems discussed in this chapter.

What's more? Having acquired this book and the information it contains, you've given yourself a considerable edge over your competitors who intend to start a dropshipping business without adequate knowledge or preparation – they just hope to wing it.

Did You Know

70% of online shoppers prioritize zooming in on images before purchasing. Are your images all optimized for web and easy to see?

Chapter 4

How to Start Your Own Dropshipping Business

Alright, now that you know what you are getting into, let's now discuss how you can actually start your own dropshipping business from scratch. I'll need you to pay close attention because we'll be discussing the basic framework with regards to starting a dropshipping business. I suggest that you read every word in this chapter if you are a complete beginner. When you look into the dropshipping business model, it seems so simple. It's almost too simple to a fault. But don't let that trick you into thinking that the journey is going to be easy. Underestimating the journey ahead is one of the biggest mistakes that aspiring entrepreneurs often mistake.

Before You Even Begin

I need you to do me a favor. Before you start building your own dropshipping business, I need you to make a promise to yourself that you are in it for the long run. As I have said a few times already, dropshipping is not a get-rich-quick scheme. So I need you to get rid of this type of thinking. I want you to be in it because you want to build something that is going to be sustainable in months and years to come. I'm telling you this out of my personal experience. When I first started dropshipping, I was in a hurry to find success and I wanted to make as much money as I could then move on to something else.

Needless to say, I wasn't successful in my first attempts at dropshipping. I made so many mistakes. Looking back, it's so clear to me now how those mistakes caused me to fail numerous times. Hopefully, with this book, I'll be able to teach people how to avoid those mistakes. I don't want you making the same mistakes I made. I don't want you to lose money the way I lost money because I was blinded by promises of instant profits. I just want you to start with a good business foundation.

The Mindset Required to Succeed

When it comes to mindset, you should be focused on achieving your goals no matter what. It doesn't matter how big or small your goals are, you should laser-focus your efforts and attention on them. Everything you do should be about taking steps toward those goals. Before you do anything, you ask yourself the following question: will this take me a step closer towards achieving my goal? If the answer is yes, then keep doing it. If the answer is no, then you should stop whatever you're doing and refocus. With regards to commitment, it's helpful if you are as committed as you are focused. Commitment means putting all your effort into the business. You go the extra mile if you have to. Never ever procrastinate. Don't put off for tomorrow what you can do today.

Where Do You Start?

To begin your dropshipping business, you have to do your assignment and that is to educate yourself about the business and the industry. Learn everything you can about dropshipping. That includes reading this book from page one to the last. I want you to read other books on dropshipping if necessary. I am not that self-centered to think that I have the answer to every question you have. Please do your assignment. Read blogs on dropshipping. Read websites on dropshipping. Browse through forums that tackle dropshipping topics. Dropshipping is just like any business. You have better chances in succeeding if you are knowledgeable about the industry's ins and outs.

After Educating Yourself, What's Your Next Move?

Okay, so you've done your assignment. You've done your research on how dropshipping works and how the model operates. Your mind is full of ideas, data, statistics, and other necessary information. Now what? Well, it's time to jump into the bandwagon and get started. It's time to get your hands dirty. To make this chapter easy to read and digest, I've decided to write it in the form of a step-by-step guide. Simply follow the steps and you will always be on the right track. So here we go!

Step 1: Make Sure That You Have Everything You Need

So the obvious question is this: what are the things you need to start a dropshipping business? There is no definitive answer to this question because every dropshipping business is unique. This means that different dropshipping businesses have different needs and requirements. However, there are the main requirements that should be present in every dropshipping business. These are as follows:

- ➢ The product or products.
- ➢ Capital.
- ➢ Website.
- ➢ Supplier or manufacturer.
- ➢ An ordering and payment system specifically designed for the dropshipping model.
- ➢ A method of receiving money (i.e. PayPal, Payoneer, money transfer, credit cards, or direct bank transfer)

These are the most basic things you need to get started. Each of these are discussed in more depth in other chapters in this book so I'm not going to expand on them in this particular chapter.

Step 2: Decide on the Products That You Are Going to Sell

What's great about the dropshipping business model is that you can sell almost every type of product. As long as it can be safely and legally shipped, it's up for grabs. The two most important factors you need to consider when deciding which products to sell are demand and competition. There should be enough online demand for the product for your business to be profitable. And the competition shouldn't be too tough in the sense that it won't be very difficult for you to take a piece of the market. So the formula in deciding what products to sell is as follows:

High Demand + Low Competition = Profitable Product

But how will you know if there's high demand or if there's low competition surrounding a product. This is where your research skills come into play. You have to do a lot of researching to determine the profitability of a product. Fortunately, there are a lot of tools and resources online that can help you with your research. You should not take this step lightly. Many aspiring online entrepreneurs go with their instincts and most of them will fail. Don't make the same mistake. Every decision you make should be backed up by data and statistics. This is why I keep on reiterating the importance of doing research and finding out as much as you can about the products that you are going to sell.

You need to focus your attention on a specific niche. Finding a niche and selecting the products to sell are discussed in more detail in Chapter Seven. The biggest reason why you should focus your efforts on a particular niche is that it's easier to compete which means you have better chances of being successful. It's also easier to get an accurate measurement of the demand for products in a niche.

Again, to determine demand and competition for a product, you should make use of online tools like keyword tools, trend spotters, and search metrics. So far, the best keyword research tool out there is Google's Keyword Tool. It offers much more accurate information and data. This is not surprising given the fact that Google controls more than 60% of the search market. The keyword tool is free to use so you there's absolutely no reason why you shouldn't use it. If you have a Gmail account, that's all you need to log into the keyword tool and start using its various features and functions. Other notable keyword tools are Merchant Words and KeywordTool IO

When doing your research, keep an eye on keywords that get a lot of searches but with very little competition. These keywords don't have to be product-related. If they are popular enough, maybe you can think of a product that you can tie into it. That's why using a keyword research tool is very important. It opens doors and introduces you to product ideas that you normally wouldn't think of on your own.

Step 3: Decide on the Business Structure That You Want to Pursue

In order to maximize your revenue and protect yourself from lawsuit, it can be advantageous to run your business with a company. You have several options. You can either register your business as a sole proprietorship, a limited liability company (LLC), or a C corporation. These are the three most commonly used business structures. It's important that you are completely aware of the differences between these business types - their pros and cons, so to speak. There are a lot of factors that you must take into account in deciding whether it would be better to register your new business as a sole proprietorship or as any of the other business types. Such factors include your business plan, business model, the possible tax advantages, the level of structure and formality, your business goals, your sources of investment, and where you want to conduct your business.

Most experienced dropshippers will tell you that it's best for you to choose between sole proprietorship and limited liability company (LLC). Although a C Corporation is still a great choice depending on the nature of your planned business. Below is a quick rundown of these three business structures.

> **Sole Proprietorship** – This business structure is the easiest to implement but you have to always keep in mind that it does not offer you much protection against personal liability. You are in danger of losing your personal assets in the event that your business get sued. Many dropshippers choose the sole proprietorship business structure because it has very minimal filing requirements. When it comes to reporting your earnings from the business, all you have to do is report the earnings under your personal taxes. That's it. No other federal or state business filings are required from you.

> **Limited Liability Company (LLC)** – This business structure establishes your business as a separate legal entity from you. This means that it provides better protection for all your personal assets. Simply put, it offers much better protection compared to that offered by a sole proprietorship. However, you should take note that this protection is neither foolproof nor absolute. Furthermore, in most instances, you will be required to comply with additional filings. You will also be paying for incorporation fees and ongoing fees.

> **C Corporation** – When it comes to protection against liabilities, a C Corporation business structure offers the most comprehensive protection. But this increased protection comes at a cost. First of all, it is much more expensive to start a business with this structure. The business will also likely be subjected to double taxation. This is because income from the

business does not pass directly to the shareholders. Instead, they can be accessed via dividends, which are taxed separately after corporation tax.

I highly advise that you consult with a lawyer, accountant or a business consultant to help you decide which structure is *best suited to you* and your business needs. Get their thoughts and recommendations before you make any incorporation decisions. Majority of small businesses go with either an LLC or a sole proprietorship. Many go with an LLC because it provides a good trade-off with regards to personal liability protection, costs, and autonomy from personal finances.

What You Need to Know About Incorporating Outside of the United States

What if you are located outside the United States but you still want to create a Limited Liability Company or a C Corporation under US laws and jurisdiction? Here's how you should go about it. It's not as difficult as you might think. These are the core steps you should follow:

1. Choose your business structure.
2. Choose a state to incorporate or file your LLC in.
3. Get a registered agent.
4. Get an employer identification number (EIN).
5. Open a U.S. business bank account (e.g. via Payoneer)
6. Get the advice of a business consultant or any knowledgeable professional.
7. Stay compliant with the rules and regulations.

Step 4: Get Your Finances in Order

The amount of money you need to invest in the business depends on several factors. These factors include the size of your planned business, the overall price of the products you are selling, the location of your supplier or manufacturer, the software and programs you use on your dropshipping website, and projected overhead costs. Take all of these factors into account to ensure that you come up with a realistic estimate for your finances. You need to make sure that you have enough funds to get started. You also need to make projections of your costs and expenses in a time period of at least one year.

Ways to Finance Your Dropshipping Business

1. **Self-Funding**: You finance the business yourself. That is all business expenses will be covered by you alone.

2. **Crowdfunding**: This is a good option if you don't have enough savings to cover the projected costs of starting and building your business. Crowdfunding sites you can consider include:
   - Kickstarter
   - Indiegogo
   - Crowd Supply
   - Crowdfunder
   - Experiment
   - Chuffed
   - Patreon
   - Fundable
   - Wefunder
   - SeedInvest
   - Fundly
   - LendingClub
   - StartSomeGood
   - Crowdcube
   - Funding Circle

3. **Small Business Loan**: Applying for a loan with the Small Business Administration or SBA is a great choice if you have a good personal credit rating. Your credit rating is among the things that the SBA will take into consideration. It is also required that you present clear copies of your business plan and financial projections. If your application is compelling, the SBA might grant you with a low-interest loan. I highly recommend that you go over your presentation numerous times. You should also consult with a business advisor to ensure that your talking points and data for the presentation are accurate and correct.

4. **Bootstrapping**: This refers to the practice of funding your business operations from money you have at hand and from the profits you make from the business. Every dollar that your business earns is put back into the business. You don't incur debts and you get to build your business at a balanced and controlled pace.

5. **Local Investors**: These are prominent people in your area who have a knack for investing in local businesses. They usually provide you with the funds you need in exchange for a share of the profits or some equity in the business.

It is also important that you learn how to separate your personal expenses from your business expenses. You do this by opening new accounts under the name of your business. Your business should always be a separate entity from your personal life. There should be a clear boundary between the two especially during the early stages of your business. There are a lot of reasons why your personal expenses should be completely separate from your business expenses. One, it's easier to account for the expenses and costs that are related to your business. Two, it's much easier to track where your funds are going. Three, it will be easier for the IRS to audit your documents. And last but not the least, it protects you from liability on business debts. If there is no clear distinction between your personal and business finances, then your creditors have a better position in going after your personal assets to offset the debts.

Your business should have separate accounts for the following:

- ✓ **Business Checking Account** – When creating a checking account for your business, your ultimate goal should be to use it for all your business finances. All you really need is one primary checking account. All of your expenses should be withdrawn from the account. It also follows that all your profits will be deposited back into the account. One obvious benefit of this setup is that it makes accounting much easier for your business. The trails of your expenses and revenues are much clearer thus easier to follow and track.

- ✓ **PayPal Account** – When you sign up with PayPal, you have three types of accounts to choose from. These are Personal, Premier, and Business. If you are going to use PayPal for cash inflows and outflows in your dropshipping business, then you should sign up using a Business account. Don't worry, you can always create a Personal account that's completely separate from your Business account. Just make sure that you don't mingle your finances using the two accounts.

- ✓ **Business Debit/Credit Card** – It's never a good idea to use your personal debit/credit card for business expenses and for purchasing inventories from a supplier. So what you need to do is set up a business credit card or debit card that is used *solely* for your business expenses. If you want recommendations about which credit cards are best for dropshipping businesses, I suggest that you consider Capital One, American Express, and Fidelity Visa.

How Much Money Are You Going to Need to Start a Dropshipping Business?

Good question. Unfortunately, there is no definitive answer. There are a lot of factors that determine how much funds you need to start your business. These include the selling price of your products, the number of products you expect to move, the location of your supplier, the cost of acquiring the necessary sales software for your business, the cost of building your website, the cost of hiring a web designer and developer, the cost of hiring a customer support operator, the cost of registering your business, the expenses you spend on consultants, and so on and so forth. The expenses and costs associated with these factors vary greatly. This means that the funds you need to start your business could be as low as $500 or as high as one million dollars.

It can be very difficult to track all of your expenses and costs especially if you do not have a background or experience in accounting or bookkeeping. For this reason, I highly recommend that you hire an accountant to keep track of your cash inflows and outflows. You don't have to hire him to work as a full-time employee. There are thousands of freelance accountants and bookkeepers out there so this shouldn't be a problem. Aside from keeping records and making your finances easy to understand, the accountant can also help you in making major business decisions based on the financial health of your business. Furthermore, there are plenty of online accounting software you can get to help you with bookkeeping e.g. Quickbooks.

Step 5: Request for an EIN Number

The Internal Revenue Service or IRS requires all types of businesses with principal operations in the United States or U.S. Territories to apply for an EIN (Employer Identification Number). The EIN serves as a social security number for your dropshipping business. You are going to use this number when filing your taxes, opening a bank account, applying for wholesale dropshipping accounts, and pretty much anything that's related to the operation of your business. You have to keep in mind that majority of reputable dropship suppliers will ask you for an EIN if you want to do business with them. If you don't have an EIN number, it will be difficult for you to find good dropship suppliers.

To start requesting for an EIN number, you need to get a copy of the application form which is the IRS Form SS-4. You can download this form from the official website of the IRS. Just print out a copy of the application form then answer all the questions therein. If you need help in completing the application form, you should get in touch with a lawyer or a business adviser.

4 Ways to Request for an EIN Number

1. **Apply Online** – You can only apply online if you have a valid tax identification number. Go to the official IRS website and look for the section called EIN Assistant. This is where you input and submit your data. After completing and submitting the form online, the system will verify and validate the information. If the form is deemed correct and error-free, you can receive an EIN immediately.

2. **Apply by Fax** – After completing your IRS Form SS-4, you send it via fax to your state fax number. Don't forget to include your own fax number in your submission. You should be able to get a response within four business days. Receiving your EIN number this way is slower compared to when you apply online.

3. **Apply by Snail Mail** – Although I don't recommend this method of requesting for an EIN number, it's still a good method especially if it's the only option you have. You fill up the form then send it to the appropriate IRS office depending on the state where you are located. Your EIN number will also arrive at your place via snail mail within four weeks. That's a whole month.

4. **Apply by Telephone** – To get an EIN number via phone, all you have to do is call the Business and Specialty Tax Line at (800) 829-4933. You can call them on weekdays from 7:00 am until 10:00 pm. An IRS representative will ask you for all your information and if things go smoothly, the representative should be able to assign you a EIN number at the end of the phone conversation.

Step 6: Get Your Sales Taxes in Order

Because of its business model, paying taxes for goods sold via dropshipping is more complicated than you might expect. The process is made complicated by issues of dropshipper location, customer location, product sourcing, and sales tax nexus. Nexus is a legal term which refers to the requirement for businesses conducting business in a state to collect and pay taxes on sales originating from the same state. For instance, if you sell goods in Houston, then you must file and pay state taxes in Texas. It's not that difficult to see why dropshipping is a business model that carries a very high risk for sales tax errors.

The biggest question here is when is it required for you to collect sales taxes? Here's a quick overview of the information you need to know about collecting and paying sales taxes in a dropshipping business:

- ✓ You have to collect sales from the customer if you have nexus in the state where the sale occurred. (Please refer to our definition for "nexus" above.) You need to collect sales tax unless the transaction is considered as tax-exempt.
- ✓ If you and your supplier don't have nexus in the state where the transaction occurred, then you are not obligated to collect sales tax. It is the customer who is obligated to remit tax unless the sale is deemed to be exempt from tax.
- ✓ If you don't have nexus in the state where the sale happened but your supplier does, then it's possible that your supplier is the one responsible for collecting sales tax. However, this is not an absolute rule considering the fact that many states have different takes on the matter. For example, states like Hawaii, Florida, Connecticut, and California hold the supplier responsible for collecting sales tax in this scenario. But many other states don't hold the same position. With that said, it's important that you check the tax laws in your state. Not all states consider drop shipping as a nexus-creating activity.

I know, it can be very confusing. So I highly recommend that you consult with a tax expert and explain your business operations so that he can advise you on whether you are required to collect sales taxes or not. Get the advice of someone who knows the business and tax laws in your own state. In a nutshell, you are going to collect sales tax if:

- ✓ The state you operate from requires you to collect sales tax and
- ✓ The customer who bought the product is located in your state.

Step 7: Make Sure That Everything Is Ready to Go

You are now at the final stages of launching your dropshipping business. All you need to do now is review everything to make sure that they are in place and are ready to go. What some online entrepreneurs do is perform a beta test of their business. That is they launch a test version of their dropshipping website. This is a good way to determine if the features and functions of your website are functioning properly. Get a friend or someone you know to order from your website and see what happens.

You should create a checklist of your website's features and functions so that you can check them one by one if they are working properly. Is the buy button clickable? Is the checkout section working smoothly? Are the payment options in place? Are the product photos displaying properly? These are just some of the questions you need to ask yourself when reviewing your dropshipping website. You have to take note of the amount of time it takes for your supplier to ship the product to the customer. If you promised delivery within three days on your website but the product arrived after more than five days, then there's a problem. You need to talk with your supplier and review your shipping details.

Before launching the business, verify and confirm with your suppliers if they have the inventories ready. It would be a shame if you launch your business but then it turns out that the supplier doesn't have enough inventory or doesn't have any inventory at all. The amount of inventory you order from your supplier should be based on your sales projections. In fact, you should order a little bit more than your sales projections to account for potential surges in sales. For example, let's say that you project to sell 1000 products in your first week. To prepare for the possibility that you might get sales that are beyond this projection, you can instruct your supplier to have an inventory of 1200 to 1500 products.

Step 8: Create a Comprehensive Marketing Plan

This is the final step before you launch your dropshipping business. Marketing is everything when it comes to running an online business. You have to learn how to put your products in front of your target customers. In ecommerce, a high-quality product amounts to nothing if nobody knows about it. What you need to do is write a comprehensive marketing plan which details how you are going to promote your business and your products. It will serve as your guide once you launch your business. This is very important especially if your business is in a really competitive niche.

Writing a marketing plan is not that difficult. If you are clueless as to how you should start, you can try searching for marketing plan templates online. There are dozens of these templates out there that you can download. Some were even specifically written for dropshipping businesses. A marketing plan is basically a blueprint for you and your marketing team. With that said, make sure that everything inside the marketing plan is realistic and actionable. Don't make lofty goals if it's going to be nearly impossible to achieve them. A marketing plan can be a few pages short or dozens of pages long. It all depends on the size and nature of your business.

In writing the marketing plan, don't forget to address the following strategies in online marketing:
- Search engine optimization or SEO
- Social media marketing (Facebook, Twitter, Instagram, WhatsApp, Snapchat, Pinterest, Reddit)
- Content marketing (article marketing, guest blogging, freelance writing, press releases)
- Advertising (direct advertising, advertising programs, Adsense)
- Video marketing (YouTube, Vimeo)
- Blogging,
- Solo Ads (i.e. renting email lists),
- Banner ads (placed on websites where your target customers congregate) etc.

These are the most common and most effective strategies in promoting products online. I suggest that you implement most if not all of them initially to figure out which option works best for you and then work with them in order to maximize your market reach. The more you put yourself out there, the more attention and hype you build towards your business. There is no such thing as over-marketing. Make it your goal to connect with your target customers in as many platforms as possible. Yes, it's going to be very time-consuming, not to mention expensive, but it's going to be worth it if you play your cards right. Marketing is something you should be doing every single day if you want your dropshipping business to be as successful as you have envisioned.

There's one last advice I'm going to offer you with regards to creating a marketing plan. And that is to make your marketing plan flexible and adaptable to changes. When you finally launch your business and you kick off your marketing campaign, you are going to realize sooner or later that some marketing strategies aren't suitable for your business. For example, you realize that your customers aren't keen on connecting with you on social media. Or you realize that not many people read blogs about the products you are selling. Your marketing plan should be adaptable in the sense that you can revise it as you go depending on the effectiveness of the methods you are using.

Step 9: Launch the Business

This is it! This is the moment you have been waiting for. It's time to launch your business and make it official. This is the easiest step in the process of starting a dropshipping business provided that you've completed all of the earlier steps. What's great about launching an online business is that you don't have to spend a ton of money or create fake fanfare to do it. In fact, it's just like any of the days leading up to the launching. You just log into the proper accounts connected to your business and make the business live. You don't have to worry about stuff like ribbon cuttings, inviting guest, etc.

You have to be prepared for the contingencies associated with an online business launch. This is why you need to be very vigilant during the first several days. Anything can go wrong with your website. It can crash due to an overwhelming amount of traffic. It can become inaccessible for hours at a time. Customers may find some of the features and functions not working properly. Customers may not be able to complete their orders. These are just a few of the potential problems that can occur in the early days of your operations. Don't worry, problems like these are quite common for new online entrepreneurs. As I said earlier, you have to be prepared for them. Instruct your technical team and customer support to be extra alert.

Chapter Summary

As you can see, starting a dropshipping business is not a walk in the park. Granted it can be easy once you've established a rhythm and you know what you're doing. However, at the beginning it can be a challenge – especially if you're not well prepared. It requires focus and patience from you. The step-by-step guide I have provided you in this chapter are but a basic framework of the process. Under each step are more steps that you need to complete. As you go through each step, you will encounter issues that may have not been discussed in this chapter. That's okay. No book can ever completely anticipate what you are going to face when you start your dropshipping business. This is why I've mentioned several times in this book that you need to take things slowly. Don't rush because you might make mistakes that you can't undo. Going through this book will help you understand the potential pitfalls and help you correctly anticipate them. You will be proactive instead of reactive.

Did You Know

90% of customers buying decisions are influenced by online reviews. Do you have the right e-commerce data analytics that consolidates and presents all your online reviews for you to take action on?

Chapter 5

How The Supply Chain and Fulfillment Process Works

A good understanding of how the supply chain and fulfillment process works is very important if you are planning to run a dropshipping business. After all, you have to learn how a plane works before you will be able to fly it. That being said, how the supply chain and fulfillment process works is not that hard to understand. There's a slight variation in the process if you are in the dropshipping industry because of the higher number of key players involved. In this chapter, we are going to discuss these key players and their roles in the supply chain and fulfillment process. We'll also discuss them in the context of a dropshipping business model.

But before anything else, let's define what a "supply chain" is. This is but a fancy term used to describe the path which a product takes from conception, to manufacturing, and then into the hands of the intended customer. There are several key players involved in this supply chain and they are as follows:

Manufacturers

This is where the supply chain starts. Manufacturers or producers make the products but in most cases, they are not the ones who sell the items to consumers. Instead, what they do is sell their goods to either wholesalers or retailers. Needless to say, if you are a reseller, cutting out the middleman and buying directly from the manufacturer is the cheapest way to get the products and you get to keep more of the profit margin. However, it's not that simple because most manufacturers require minimum purchases. For example, you need 100 units of the products but the manufacturer requires a minimum purchase of 500 units. As a reseller, you also need to stock the products and then ship them if you are selling these to consumers. Because of these reasons, many entrepreneurs prefer purchasing their products from wholesalers.

Wholesalers

Wholesalers do not produce the goods themselves. What they do is purchase the products in bulk from the manufacturers then sell them to retailers for resale to consumers. Wholesalers earn money by putting a markup on the bulk orders they purchase from manufacturers. For example, let's say Brock is a wholesaler and Cain is a manufacturer. Brock makes a bulk order of 1000 product units from Cain for $1 each. Brock then resells the products to retailers with a markup of 10 cents per unit. If Brock is able to sell the whole bulk to retailers, then he has gross profits amounting to $100 (1000 units multiplied by 0.10).

Wholesalers usually have lower minimum purchase requirements compared to manufacturers. This is understandable given the fact that they don't make the goods themselves. Because they are not into production, wholesalers often purchase products from dozens or hundreds of manufacturers and stock the goods in their own warehouses. Furthermore, wholesalers tend to operate within specific niches and industries. That is they sell a wide range of products but such products belong to the same niche. For example, a wholesaler stocks a wide range of products in the footwear industry (i.e. shoes, sandals, socks) from dozens of manufacturers. Generally, wholesalers don't sell directly to the public. They only sell to retailers.

Retailers

As a dropshipper, this is where you belong. If you purchase products from manufacturers or wholesalers then resell these to the public at a markup, then you are the very definition of a retailer. However, there's a slight variation in the process because you are not the one shipping the products. That responsibility lies in the hands of your supplier. Here's what's interesting if you look at these three players in the context of the dropshipping model. All three of them can be dropshippers. A manufacturer can have a dropshipping operation in-house, a wholesaler can be a dropshipper, and a retailer can be a dropshipper.

Consumers

Customers who order and pay for goods complete the supply chain and fulfillment process. Once the customer receives the product he ordered, it means it has been fulfilled and the process is complete.

The Dropshipping Process in Action

To best understand how the dropshipping process works, I'm going to provide you with an example. We are going to look into the steps necessary to complete a dropshipped order. Let's say that you own a dropshipping business called Smith Company. You sell customized shirts that you order from a wholesaler called Bravo Company. Here's how the process works:

Step 1: Customer orders a shirt from Smith Company.
- A customer named Jerry comes across the website of Smith Company, browses through the products listed, and decides to place an order for a nice shirt. Once the order goes through, Jerry will receive an email confirming his purchase. Jerry's payment will also be captured by the website's checkout system and deposited in Smith Company's bank account.

Step 2: Smith Company sends the order to Bravo Company, the wholesaler and supplier.

- With an automated system, Smith Company's website will simply send the customer order or email the order confirmation to Bravo Company. A sales representative at Bravo Company reviews the order, checks if Smith Company is on their file of retailers, then starts processing the order. With the cost of goods, shipping fees, and processing fees taken into account, Bravo Company then bills Smith Company for the order.

Step 3: Bravo Company ships the product to Jerry, the customer.

- Assuming that Bravo Company has the ordered product in stock and that they were able to bill Smith Company's account, they then put the shirt in a box and ship it directly to Jerry's address. Although the boxed shirt is coming from Bravo Company, the return address is still that of Smith Company. The invoice and packing slip will also contain the details of Smith Company, not that of Bravo Company. After finalizing the shipment, Bravo Company then sends an invoice as well as a tracking number to Smith Company.

Step 4: Smith Company informs Jerry that the shirt he ordered has been shipped and is on its way.

- After receiving the invoice and tracking number from Bravo Company, Smith Company then forwards the tracking number to Jerry. Jerry will use the tracking number as verification when the boxed shirt is delivered to his residence or office. Once Jerry receives the item, then the order has been fulfilled. Smith Company's profit from the process is the difference between the price it charged Jerry and the price it paid Bravo Company to ship the product. For instance, let's say Smith Company sold the shirt to Jerry for $20 and it paid Bravo Company $15 to handle and ship the item. That means Smith Company earned a gross profit of $5 from the sale.

Chapter Summary

The dropshipping model seems easy enough from the surface but it can be very complicated once you are in the thick of the business. Our illustration and example above is just the tip of the iceberg. There are so many other things happening in between the four steps. Furthermore, there are also a lot of errors that can happen in between the steps. Packages can get lost or damaged in transit. Since the packages have a return address containing the details of Smith Company, it's Smith Company who will receive the complaints and requests for returns and replacements. Smith Company ships the damaged or defective products back to Bravo Company and make another request for replacements. In short, there are many parties involved so it's often harder to manage a dropshipping business compared to a standard ecommerce business. A good way to minimize the return rate is to be strategic with your product selections i.e. deal with simple products that are not easily breakable. For example, dropshipping a tennis ball or T-shirt is far less challenging than dropshipping ceramic plates. Of course, first and foremost, make sure there's strong demand for the product and its not too competitive.

Did You Know

33% of UK online sales occur after 6pm. Are you targeting correctly?

Other Notable Books By Michael Ezeanaka	
Book #	**Book Title**
1	Affiliate Marketing Made Easy
2	55 Passive Income Ideas Analysed
3	Amazon FBA Mastery
4	Dropshipping
5	Real Estate Investing For Beginners
6	Credit Card Mastery
7	Facebook Advertising Made Easy
8	Stock Market Investing For Beginners
The kindle edition will be available to you for FREE when you purchase the paperback version from Amazon.com (The US Store)	

Chapter 6

Evaluating Your Sales Channels

One of the biggest benefits of a dropshipping business is that you have access to several sales channels. After deciding which products to sell, securing your suppliers, and establishing your business legally, the next step is to decide how you are going to put your products in front of your target customers. These are called sales channels. The good news is that you have several channels to choose from. You can also try to use more than one sales channels at a time. As long as you have the time and the resources to use several channels, by all means go for it. It's advisable that you slowly go through each of these channels, look into their pros and cons, before deciding which of them you are going to use.

I) Dropshipping on eBay

eBay is an institution in itself, which is why a lot of dropshippers make use of the platform. The company has been around for more than two decades, which means they have proven themselves to be sustainable since they were able to last that long. And there is the fact that eBay is without a doubt the world's largest auction site as far as physical goods are concerned.

The Pros of Selling on eBay

1. It's easy to get started. With the platform, you can simply create an account and start listing your products. You can be in business in under an hour.
2. Access to a really large audience. eBay has millions of active buyers from all over the world. If you list your products properly, it has the potential of being seen by millions of potential customers.
3. It requires less marketing. That is if you compare it with other lesser known online auction platforms. Let's call a spade a spade. In listing a product on eBay, you are piggybacking on the site's enormous popularity. You don't have to worry that much about paying for traffic, search engine optimization (SEO), or marketing in general. This means that eBay will save you a lot of time. Let's face it, marketing is one of the biggest challenges associated with starting a dropshipping business.

The Cons of Selling on eBay

1. You have to pay for listing fees. There are two main types of fees that you have to pay when you list and sell a product on eBay. The first one is the insertion fee. When you list a product for sale, eBay will charge you an insertion fee per listing and per category. This means that if you list a single product to two categories, you are going to pay for the

insertion fee twice. The second fee is the final value fee (sometimes referred to as the success fee). The final value fee can be up to 10% or even higher of the sales price of the product you listed.

2. It's very difficult to customize your product listings. This is a huge disadvantage especially if you want to differentiate your products on the platform. Every listing you make should follow eBay's template. This makes it really hard to create a more professional-looking listing that adds value to your products.

3. You need to be constantly monitoring, tracking, and re-listing your products on eBay. Always keep in mind that eBay has an auction-style platform. If the auction period runs out, the item has to be relisted. Just imagine how much work this will be if you have numerous product listings. Of course, there are some tools that you can use to automate the process or outsource it to virtual assistants.

II) Dropshipping on Amazon

Amazon is the largest online marketplace out there so it makes complete sense to consider it for your dropshipping business. However, before you start using Amazon as your sales channel, make sure that you've read the company's policies on dropshipping. You can read the policies when you log into your Amazon Seller account. For example, Amazon requires you to identify yourself as the seller in all the packing slips and other information associated with your products.

The Pros of Selling on Amazon

1. You deal with much lower overhead. You can forget about things like stocking, shipping, storing, and ordering. You can just focus your time on passing the orders you receive to your supplier.
2. You have immediate access to a huge market. Millions of people shop on Amazon every single day. This means your product listings have the potential of being seen by a lot of people provided that you optimized your listings.
3. You will save a lot of money and resources on shipping because you don't have to do it.
4. You don't have to worry about a limited product inventory because no one is stopping you from listing dozens of products on Amazon. As long as you have your suppliers and manufacturers in place, everything should go fine.
5. You have access to a lot of features and functions provided by Amazon's selling platform. These include tracking systems that enable you to collect and analyse data about your product listings and their corresponding sales figures.

6. Amazon allows you to dropship larger items. Again, you are not handling and shipping the products yourself so you have nothing to be worried about. You just have to make sure that your suppliers keep their end of the bargain.

The Cons of Selling on Amazon

1. You are under the mercy of Amazon. They can shut down your account for the slightest infraction. There's really no flexibility for you to do things on your own. In a sense, you are making money not just for yourself but for Amazon as well. This means that the fruits of your labor are divided between you and the retail giant.

2. You don't have access to customer data. You have access to stats about the sales but nothing about the customers themselves. This is unlike running your own dropshipping website wherein you can gather data about your customers.

3. It's hard to find suppliers who will agree to dropship for you through Amazon. Most suppliers prefer working directly with dropshippers because if Amazon is involved, that's another party that takes a cut in the overall profits.

4. Your hard work can disappear overnight. If your listings or your account gets compromised, you have to go through the appeal process which can take days and even weeks. Good if you get your account back but what if Amazon decides to ban it for good?

III) Dropshipping on Shopify

Shopify has become synonymous with dropshipping because the company has been specifically designed to cater to dropshippers. Shopify is now the largest dropshipping platform today. Shopify has done the hard work for you so that you don't have to build your dropshipping business from scratch. The company provides you with the tools and resources you need to run and manage your dropshipping business. For that reason, anyone can start a business using Shopify.

The Pros of Selling on Shopify

1. The platform is friendly to newbies who have zero experience in dropshipping. Shopify even has a lot of articles, guides, and tutorials on how to use the platform.

2. Built-in speed and security for hosting. In online commerce, security is crucial because there is always the risk that a hacker will hack through your website and steal anything he likes. Fortunately, Shopify has a lot of measures installed to avoid this from happening.

3. You get all the necessary features to run a dropshipping business. Whether you want to integrate a payment method or you simply want to customize the look of your store, Shopify has the tools and resources you need to make it happen.

4. Efficient customer support. This is one of the great things about Shopify. You can seek support any time of the day or night. You can reach customer service through phone, email, and online live chat.

5. You have access to a large app store. There are dozens of apps which you can use to extend the functionality of your store. Most of these apps are subscription-based but there are some which are free to use.

6. You can choose from hundreds of free and paid themes for your ecommerce store. These are themes that were made by a team of in-house and freelance designers.

The Cons of Selling on Shopify

1. Shopify charges a transaction fee for every sale, and this is on top of the monthly fee you have to pay the company for using its dropshipping platform.

2. Your monthly costs may add up if you are using multiple apps in your store. Keep in mind that most of the apps in the Shopify App Store are not free. If several of the apps you use are subscription-based, you will be paying a lot of monthly fees on top of your Shopify subscription and transaction fees.

3. Shopify has a lock-in feature which means that if you ever decide to cancel your account, your store and all your data will be permanently deleted. In short, transitioning to a new store is not going to be smooth.

IV) Alternative Sales Channels

Amazon, eBay, and Shopify are by far the most common platforms for building a dropshipping business. But you still have other options in the event that you don't want to use any of the three. One, you can always build your own online store if you have the technical and programming skills to do it. The main drawback of this method is that you have to build everything from scratch. Building your own store however offers several advantages like more control over the business, less third-party fees, and flexibility for growth.

If you don't want to build your online store from scratch either, you can explore other sales channels such as the following: Facebook Shop, Wanelo, Lazada, Pinterest, etc.

Chapter Summary

You have several options as far as your sales channels are concerned. In short, there is no shortage of platforms where you can sell your dropshipped products. Be careful about the sales channels that you use. Make sure that the channels are a good fit for the types of products you are selling. Keep in mind that just because a product sells well on Amazon doesn't necessarily mean it will also sell well on eBay or Shopify. No one is stopping you from using all the sales channels discussed in this chapter.

However, based on experience, it's best to focus your attention on a single channel. This way, you can direct all your efforts and resources into the business. The problem with using several channels at once is that it divides your time and attention. But if you have the time, the resources, as well as extra manpower to use all sales channels, then by all means, go for it.

Did You Know

It is preferred that you show the shipping costs at the very beginning or display it with the price of the product. 34% of the customers have been known to abandon their shopping carts if the shipping costs are shown late in checkout.

Please Kindly Review This Book

If you have found any value from reading this book, please kindly post a review letting us know about it. It'll only take a minute of your time. Thank you so much!

Chapter 7

Niche Research and Product Selection

Niche research and product selection are among the most important steps in building a successful dropshipping business. There are no other ways around them. You have to do them if you want to increase your chances for achieving sustained profitability. I'm telling you right now that niche research takes time and effort. It can take you days or even weeks to zero in on products that you think will be embraced by customers. Niche research is about gathering data and gauging demand for your product ideas. In other words, it's a strategy for determining if it's worth it to pursue a product or not.

What is a Niche?

In the simplest of terms, a niche is a specific category or field in an industry. This is in business and marketing terms. For example, let's talk about the broad outdoor equipment industry. Under this industry are dozens of niches. The trail running community is a niche. The mountain climbing community is a niche. The cliff jumping community is a niche. The mountain biking community is yet another niche. And so on and so forth. Even these niches can be further broken down into even smaller niches. For example, the trail running community niche can be broken down into the marathoner's niche and the ultra marathoner's niche.

Breaking down an industry into niches makes it a lot easier for aspiring entrepreneurs to find potential markets they can tap into. It allows you to look for niches that have less competition but have considerable demand. These are the two factors that you must always consider during niche research. One, the competition within the niche shouldn't be too tough in the sense that you can enter it and carve your own business in it. And two, there should be considerable demand for the products you want to offer in that niche. These two factors come hand in hand. Because what's the point of entering an uncompetitive niche if there's minimal demand for products. And what's the point of trying to fulfill a demand that's already being fulfilled by thousands of established entrepreneurs – profit margins will erode due to too much competition.

How to do Niche Research

Always remember that you have two main goals when performing niche research. One, you want to gauge demand for your product ideas. And two, you want to know the level of competition for those product ideas. You will be performing most of your research using various tools like keyword research tools and search volume trackers. Don't worry because most of these tools and resources are readily available and you can use most of them for free. Before you begin with your research, it's important that you already have an industry that you want to target. For example, you want to target the sports gear industry or the weight loss industry. I hope that you are getting my point here. The general industry serves as your starting point.

Create a Quick List of Your Product Ideas

The first thing you must do is write down a quick list of the products that you have in mind. Get a piece of paper and quickly jot down the ideas. This list will be your reference point when you start doing your research. Write down the words, phrases, and terms that come to your mind when you think about your potential products. Allow me to briefly illustrate what this list should look like. Let's say that you want to build a dropshipping business around the hiking niche. Furthermore, let's say that you want to sell hiking footwear on your dropshipping website. Brainstorming for product ideas, your initial list should look very similar to the following list:

- Hiking shoes
- Hiking sandals
- Mountain climbing shoes
- Hiking footwear
- Climbing sandals
- Durable climbing shoes
- Hiking slippers
- Tough hiking shoes
- Mountaineering shoes
- Mountaineering footwear
- Mountaineering sandals

This is just for illustration purposes. Your list can either be shorter or longer than the one above. It all depends on the products you have in mind and the niche that you want to target. My main point here is that you need to create a list of all your potential products. These should be the types of products that you plan on selling through your dropshipping website. Creating this list should take just a few minutes of your time. Some dropshippers would even divide their lists into product categories and create lists within a list. Keep a copy of this list with you as you start with your niche research.

Google Is Your Best Friend

Google controls at least 60% of all online searches so it makes sense that the search giant has the most accurate search data and statistics. Needless to say, if you want to learn about a product's popularity online, Google is where you should go for information. Google has tools that you can use for your research. The two most important ones are **Google Trends** and the **Google Keyword Tool**. Don't worry, both of these tools are free to use. You don't have to pay a dime to gain access to their features and functions. For the Keyword Tool, all you need is a Google account. If you already have a Gmail account, you can start using the Keyword Tool by simply logging into your account.

For the Google Trends tool, you don't even need a Google account to access and use it. For best results, I suggest that you use the Chrome browser when you do your research on Google Trends. Certain features of the tool tend to not work properly when you use other browsers like Mozilla Firefox. Google Trends is a very powerful research tool in the sense that you can determine search volume over time, top and rising search terms, seasonality of search terms, and even the geographical concentrations of searches. You can identify which countries are searching the most for particular products. In the following sections, I'm going to show you how to use the two tools.

How to Use Google Trends for Niche Research

Here's a quick definition of Google Trends from Wikipedia: "It is a public web facility of Google based on Google Search that shows how often a particular search term is entered relative to the total search volume across different regions in the world, and in various languages." It's basically an analytics database of all searches on Google from 2004 to the present. Needless to say, Google Trends is a goldmine for data about ecommerce niches. It contains an immense amount of search data that you can collect and analyse to determine if there's interest or demand for the products that you have in mind.

Let's take a look at the tool's specific features:

- ✓ **Interest and Search Volume Over Time** – This graphs searches based on the queries they received over time. You can quickly customize a time frame ranging from years to minutes. The graph will show you if the search volume for a particular search query is increasing or decreasing over time. It provides you with an idea if the trends will be in your favor or not. Let's say that you are planning to dropship trail running shoes. Google Trends will provide you with data if searches for the phrase "trail running shoes" is increasing or decreasing over time. If the trend shows that the number of people interested in trail running shoes is growing, then it's probably a good niche and that it's worth looking into. You can compare search data based on time periods. For example, you can compare search data this year to last year's search data. Or you can compare search data this month to last month's search data.

- ✓ **Interest by Region** – This feature enables you to pinpoint the geographical regions wherein your search term is most popular. It compares the origins of the searches. The interest data also reflects the popularity of the term in a certain region and on a certain time period. For example, you want to know more about the interest for "trail running shoes" during the first quarter of 2018. That's for the months of January, February, and March. What you do is customize the parameters in Google Trends so that it will reflect interest about "trail running shoes" during these months. The data will then show you the regions where queries for "trail running shoes" are most popular.

However, you should take note that the geographic regions are organized based on search proportions. Needless to say, some smaller countries might score much higher compared to larger countries. Interest for searches are scored by Google Trends from 0 to 100. You can determine search interest not just by country. You can further break down the interest data by states or provinces. For example, if you are doing research in the United States, you can access interest data by state.

✓ **Related Topics** – What this feature does is provide a quick list of other topics that the user also searched. Users searching for your term are also searching for these terms and topics. In our example, if you input "trail running shoes" into Google Trends, the related topics that you receive include the following topics: vapour, venture 6, sports shoes, tights, cross training, track spikes, back country running, vibram, under armour. This means that whoever is searching about trail running shoes are also interested in these general topics. How does this benefit you in your research for a niche? Well, it provides you with a ton of ideas about other products that your target market might be interested in. From our example, we can see that people searching for trail running shoes are also interested in running shorts and running spikes. These are products that you might also want to feature in your dropshipping store.

✓ **Related Queries** – A lot of people often confuse this with the Related Topics feature. The two are very different from each other. In Related Topics, you get a list of topics that the user also searched for. This means that these are general topics. In Related Queries, you are presented with a list of terms that the user also searched for. This means that people searching for your main term are also searching for these queries. In other words, these are specific queries. In our example on trail running shoes, the user also searched for the following queries: best trail running shoes 2018, black and yellow running shoes, fila trail running shoes, brooks Cascadia, zero drop running shoes, best waterproof trail running shoes, salomon speedcross 4, best trail running shoes women, and trail running shoes for hiking. These are very specific queries that the user is also searching for. Again, how will this information help you with your niche research? My answer is the same. The information helps you with more ideas about which products to promote and sell. It also provides you with ideas about other niches that you might want to further explore.

✓ **Top vs. Rising Queries** – When you look at the list of queries and topics under the Related Topics and Related Queries features, you can toggle the terms between Top and Rising. In Related Topics, the Top designation refers to the most popular topics. The Rising designation refers to topics with the largest increase in search frequency since the previous time period. In Related Queries, the Top designation refers to the most popular search queries. The Rising designation refers to search queries with the largest increase in search frequency since the previous time period. The data you gather from these features paint a picture of what's currently popular and what topics and terms have the potential to become popular.

✓ **Breakout Search Queries** – This is a feature which identifies whether a topic or a query is receiving a breakout number of searches. A topic or query is tagged as a "breakout" if there is a tremendous increase in interest and search volume for it. For example, if the search volume for "zero drop running shoes" last week was in the mere hundreds but during the current week the search volume ballooned to searches in the thousands. It will most likely be tagged as a "breakout" topic or query. However, you should be careful about breakout topics and queries because these are usually seasonal in nature. This is especially true for products that are seasonal. For example, Christmas sweaters are often tagged as breakout topics and queries weeks before Christmas day. For sure, it would be a good idea to start dropshipping Christmas sweaters but the interest will quickly die out within a month or so. If you want to build a sustainable dropshipping business that is profitable all year round, you should target products that are not seasonal in nature.

Making Sense of Google Trends as a Niche Research Tool

When you go to the Google Trends main page, just type in the term you want to do some research on. In our example, just key in the phrase "trail running shoes" into the search bar. You will be presented with an interface containing the features we just discussed above. You then customize your search based on several parameters. These parameters are as follows:

1) **Country** – Choose the specific country where you want to pull the search data from. If you want data and information from all countries, then choose the "Worldwide" option.

2) **Time Period** – You can select from any of the following options.
   ✓ Past hour
   ✓ Past 4 hours
   ✓ Past day
   ✓ Past 7 days
   ✓ Past 30 days

✓ Past 90 days
✓ Past 5 years
✓ 2004 to present
✓ Custom time range

3) **Categories** – You can select from any of the following options. If you want to gather data from all of these categories, then you should choose the "All Categories" option.

✓ All categories
✓ Arts and entertainment
✓ Autos and vehicles
✓ Beauty and fitness
✓ Books and literature
✓ Business and industrial
✓ Computers and electronics
✓ Finance
✓ Food and drink
✓ Games
✓ Health
✓ Hobbies and leisure
✓ Home and garden
✓ Internet and telecom
✓ Jobs and education
✓ Law and government
✓ News
✓ Online communities
✓ People and society
✓ Pets and animals
✓ Real estate
✓ Reference
✓ Science
✓ Shopping
✓ Sports
✓ Travel

If you choose the right parameters, then you should be provided with accurate information and data. I highly recommend that you keep a notebook with you where you can jot down important information you gather from the data presented to you. Jot down the related topics and related queries that you might want to check on later. If you are not the pen-and-paper type, you can always download the search data provided to you by Google Trends. You can download data from the following features: Interest by Region, Related Topics, and Related Queries.

How to Download the Graphs and Data from Google Trends

On the top portion of each feature are buttons signifying actions you can take. Find the one that looks like an arrow pointing downwards. This is the universal symbol for "download". If you hover over it, it says "CSV". Just click on the button to commence downloading. Downloading will take just a few seconds. To open the file, just go to your desktop's "Downloads" folder. You can also embed the graphs from Google Trends. Just click on the Embed button and you will be provided with HTML code which you can just copy and paste into any page that supports HTML.

In a nutshell, Google Trends has almost everything you need to look for a profitable niche for your dropshipping business idea. For most experienced dropshippers, Google Trends is all they need to find the next product they are going to sell. But if you are just a beginner, the data and information you collected from Google Trends may not be enough. That brings us to the Google Keyword Tool. If you are a complete newbie, I suggest that you make use of both tools in researching for your niche products.

How to Use the Google Keyword Tool for Niche Research

The Google Keyword Tool is the most popular keyword tool out there. There's no doubt about that. Almost all online marketers use the tool in one way or another. It's accurate, easy to use, and most important of all, it's completely free. To access the tool, all you need is a Google account. If you are a Gmail user, you can use the same login details to sign in into the keyword tool.

The tool has more than a dozen features and functions at your disposal. You might be confused as to why you should use the keyword tool when you already know which products to sell based on the research you've done in Google Trends. Here's what you need to understand between the two tools. Google Trends provide you with a general idea of the popularity of certain terms. The Google Keyword Tool provides you with the numbers and other specific information about the terms. The Keyword Tool allows you to determine the approximate number of searches that a term gets every week, every month, or every year.

Google has recently changed the interface for its keyword tool. It is now called the Keyword Planner and you can access it through their Google Ads program. When you click on the Keyword Planner tab, you will be directed to a window that makes you choose from two options depending on what you wish to do with the planner. The two options are as follows:

1. **Find new keywords** – This enables you to find keyword ideas that might be able to help you reach people who are interested in the products that you plan on dropshipping.

2. **Get search volume and forecasts** – With this option, you will be able to access data on search volume and other important historical metrics that are relevant to your keywords. You can also get forecasts about how your keywords might perform in the next months or years.

If it's your first time to use the Keyword Planner and you are not sure which option you should go with, I highly recommend that you read Google's comprehensive primer about the tool. When you open the Keyword Planner window, scroll down to the bottom of the page and look for the tab that says "How to Use Keyword Planner". Click on the tab and read the guide. This will provide you with the basic information you need about using the Keyword Planner. The guide is always there so you can read it whenever you want.

Find New Keywords

For beginners, this is what you should use first. All you have to do is enter the keywords you want to do research on. The next window will show a huge list of related keyword ideas, their average monthly searches, and the level of competition. There are other data present but you should focus on these three factors (keyword ideas, average monthly searches, and level of competition).

For example, if you type in "trail running shoes" in the search bar, you will receive 828 keyword ideas. That's a lot. For each keyword idea, there's corresponding data on its average monthly searches and competition level. For the keyword idea "Nike running shoes", the average monthly searches for it range from 100,000 to 1 million. The level of competition for the keyword is tagged as "high". Levels of competition in the Keyword Planner are either low, medium, or high.

Here's what you should do. Create a list of all the keyword ideas that you believe are most relevant to the product you have in mind. You should also get the data on average monthly searches and competition for each keyword. Your goal is to find keywords that are getting a good amount of searches but whose level of competition is within the low to medium range. These are the best types of keywords because they are getting a lot of searches but there are not that many websites providing content about them. Go over these keywords one at a time to remove the ones that aren't a fit for your dropshipping business idea.

Go over the keywords until you are left with 10 to 20 main keywords. The final list can even be less than 10 keywords especially if you are targeting a very small and very specific niche. Create a copy of these final keywords and keep them in your files. You can do individual analysis of each main keyword using the Keyword Planner but this is optional. It's up to you if you aren't satisfied with the list you already have.

So what are you going to do with the list of keywords you have? You are going to use it as your basis in coming up with the products that you are going to sell in your dropshipping website. The keywords will also help you in creating content for search engine optimization (SEO) purposes. It's also worth mentioning here that you can add filters when using the Keyword Planner. You have the option to exclude keywords in the results. Just click on the "Add Filter" button then type in the words and keywords you want to exclude in your research.

Get Search Volume and Forecasts

This option is specifically geared towards users who want to purchase ads from Google's advertising program. With that said, there really isn't much that you can glean from this feature if your main intention is to look for profitable keyword ideas and niches. Majority of the data and information you get about the search volume and forecasts are related to costs per click (CPC) and potential ad impressions. For example, if you want to get an ad for your website targeting the keyword "trail running shoes", the Keyword Planner forecasts that you will have to spend around $37 to get about 30,000 clicks on your advertisement.

What I am trying to say here is that the keyword ideas and competition data you need for niche research are available using the Keyword Planner's "Find New Keywords" feature. But if you want to dig deeper, you may use the "Get Search Volume and Forecasts" feature. The data here is very valuable if you have plans of buying advertisements for your dropshipping business down the line. You can get estimated costs and conversion metrics that will help you decide if purchasing ads is a good investment or not.

In a way, you can also use this feature of the Keyword Planner to gauge competition. Usually, if purchasing an ad for a keyword is expensive, it means that the competition is high for that keyword. Many entrepreneurs and online marketers are bidding for that keyword which subsequently increases the price of advertising for that keyword. Needless to say, you will get an idea about the level of competition for your targeted keywords based on the price of ads associated with them. The higher the price is for an ad featuring a keyword, the more competitive that keyword is. This is something you should always remember especially if you have plans of being aggressive with your ad buys.

Things to Look Out for When Selecting Products

Now that you have a good list of keywords related to the niche you want to enter, the next step is to zero in on the products that you are going to sell on your dropshipping website. There are several factors that you must consider, the most important of which are as follows:

1. **Price** – When dropshipping products, your prices should be competitive. It shouldn't be too high or too low. If it's too high, people will say it's overpriced. If it's too low, people will assume that your product is of low quality thus the low price. Most of the time, your customers are people who are too lazy to go out and buy the product themselves from department stores or groceries. So it's okay to dropship products at a slightly higher price compared to department store prices. Most consumers will understand the difference in the price.

When you look at the price of a product, you have to consider the markup associated with the dropshipping model. For example, if a pair of shoes you are planning to sell costs $20 on a retailer's ecommerce store, you have to assume that if you are going to dropship the same product, it will have to cost a little bit more. The markup should not be too much in the sense that the gap between your price and the other retailer's price is too much for the customer to justify.

2. **Marketing potential** – The product should be an item that can be marketed online on most promotional platforms. You should be able to promote it via social media, blogs, forums, direct advertising, content marketing, advertising programs like Adsense, podcasts, etc. Your target customers are online and the only way to reach them is through online marketing channels. For this to work, the product has to be marketable on such a platform.

3. **Lots of related accessories** – As a dropshipper, you have the option of selling accessories that are related to your main product. Accessories are a great source of additional sales and income. In fact, some dropshippers make more money from their accessories than from their main products. The term "accessory" is a rather broad term so allow me to explain it further in the context of the dropshipping business model. Let us go back to our example of dropshipping trail running shoes. Accessories that you can sell which are relevant to your main product may include the following:
   - Trail running socks
   - Shoe gaiters
   - Shoe blinkers
   - Shoe glue
   - Anti-blister socks
   - Five finger socks

Adding accessories to your ecommerce store is a great idea. They are usually a lot less expensive so they get bought much quicker. And not to mention the fact that they are easier to pack and ship. You can also try to sell accessories in bundles or packages. Use these packages to entice your target customers to purchase your main products.

4. **Low Return Rate** – It's far more strategic to deal with products that are simple in nature in order to minimize the chance of something going wrong e.g. one would expect to see a higher return

rate when dropshipping a fragile ceramic plate which is more likely to break on transit, especially if it's packaged properly. Furthermore, electronic appliances are likely to malfunction which might lead customers to return them. However, dealing with simple products like a shoe, T-shirt, tennis ball, phone leather/rubber case etc. isn't quite as risky. As a result, it's easier to meet customer expectations and you're less likely to get unsatisfied customers asking for a refund.

5. **Hard to find locally** – Look for products that are rarely sold in department stores and grocery stores in your area. This is a good strategy especially if you are planning to dropship products to a specific location. For example, if trail running shoes are difficult to find in your town or city, then it would be a good idea to set up a dropshipping business selling trail running shoes and targeting customers in your town or city.

A Quick Recap of Measuring Competition

As I have mentioned several times already, you need to gauge the competition for a product before you decide to add the item to your dropshipping business. The general consensus is that if the competition is very tough, you should abandon the idea and brainstorm for others. This is true in many levels but there is an exception. Don't abandon the idea entirely. The fact that the competition for the product is very tough means that there's a lot of money to be made with the product. What you should do is further break down the product idea into niches and find the ones with less competition. This way, you are within a competitive niche but you are targeting a product with less competition niche-wise. Doing so basically allows you to take advantage of the demand while avoiding too much competition.

Another powerful way of gauging competition is by examining the number of organically listed sites on the first page of Google. Type in your main keyword and analyse the results. If several pages of the results contain the exact keyword, then it's a very competitive niche – these many people wouldn't be running ads if there weren't money to be made. Look at the top results and think if you can compete with them. Do you think you can optimize your dropshipping website and make it rank high in the results page? Or are the top results too established that it would be nearly impossible to reach or even topple them? You have to be realistic with your analysis especially if there are a lot of big brands in the top search results. For example, you are overconfident if you think that you can compete with the likes of Nike or Adidas when it comes to selling running shoes online. They have a lot of marketing power and a sizeable budget. You have to avoid competing against the big dogs by finding your own niche.

Find a Niche Where You Can Add Value to the Product

One way of getting ahead of the competition is to add value to the products you are dropshipping. This is especially true if you are selling a generic product (one that is also being sold by countless other dropshippers). Differentiate your business by creating a unique value proposition. The next obvious question is how do you do this? One of the best ways to add value to a competitive product is to create a loyalty program for your customers. This is a great strategy if the product you are dropshipping has a high turnover rate. What you do is reward your most loyal customers in the form of discounts and promos.

Another great way of adding value to a product is to offer discounts for bulk purchases. A good example of this is a buy one take one sales model. It provides customers with a nice incentive that is too hard to refuse. Your customers will be getting more of your products at less costs. For this sales model to work, you also need to negotiate with your supplier or manufacturer for lesser costs when it comes to bulk orders. You can also arrange to bundle complementary products your customers will like to buy together e.g. a tennis ball and a racket, shoe and socks of matching brands, phones and phone cases etc.

Another method of adding value to your product is to customize its design and packaging. Beautiful packaging creates additional perceived value in the eyes of your customers. When a customer looks at your product, the very first thing they see and feel is the quality of the packaging. Having a good product design could make the whole difference between a buyer and a non-buyer. Making the product packaging as attractive as possible helps in making the customer decide to purchase the item.

Chapter Summary

Finding a profitable niche and selecting your products is a long process so you should take your time with your research. Don't rush things. You have to make sure that the data, statistics, and other information that you gather about your niche are as accurate as possible. Starting your business with bad data can be disastrous for your business. Using bad data can cause a lot of early problems like overestimating your market, picking the wrong supplier, and miscalculating the costs of running the business.

Did You Know

According to a business insider study, 23% of online shoppers fall between the ages of 35 and 44, while only 18% of the US population is that age. What are you doing to effectively target this demographic?

Chapter 8

Finding and Working With Suppliers and Manufacturers

Your dropshipping business will only be as good as the supplier and manufacturer you work with. If you have a bad supplier, it will reflect on the reputation of your business. If your supplier is always late in shipping products to your customers, it's you who is going to take the blame and criticisms. Think of your suppliers as the other half of your business operations. If they don't do their jobs properly, that means half of your business is hurting your operations. The bottom line here is that you should be serious in finding good and reliable suppliers. In this chapter, I am going to show you how you can improve your chances of snagging the right suppliers for your business.

There are so many factors that you must consider when looking for dropshipping suppliers. You need to make sure that the ones you get are reliable and trustworthy. Your ultimate goal is to find the right product from the right supplier. The good news is that there are dozens of online marketplaces out there that make this a lot easier for you. These are often referred to as wholesale and dropship directories. Some are free. Some charge a fee which could be a recurring monthly fee or a one-time fixed fee. We're going to look into some of the most popular of these wholesale and dropship directories in this chapter.

How do you find dropshipping companies and wholesalers?

The first thing you should do is subscribe to a dropshipping directory. As I stated above, there are dozens of these directories but a lot of them are low-quality and they provide little value. See to it that you only subscribe to legitimate directories. These are directories that look into the backgrounds of the companies that apply for listings. An example of a good dropshipping directory is World Wide Brands. I say they are good because they pre-screen the thousands of dropshipping companies that want to be listed in their directory.

Do extensive research about a dropshipping company before entering into a deal with them. Look into the products that they are dropshipping. Are these of good quality? Are there very little customer complaints about the products? Look for reviews about the supplier. Most dropshipping directories have review features wherein entrepreneurs can leave comments and reviews about the suppliers listed in the directory. You should be able to gauge the reliability and trustworthiness of a supplier by reading a lot of these reviews.

What are the requirements to work with a dropshipping supplier?

If your dropshipping business operates within the United States, most legitimate suppliers will require you to present them with an EIN (employer identification number). You will only get an EIN if you register your business so this is the first thing you should do. Other than this, the requirements vary depending on the supplier or wholesaler you are dealing with.

How to find legitimate wholesale suppliers:

1. Thoroughly check the supplier's profile. This is the very first thing you should do before you even think of entering into a deal with a prospective supplier. If you found the supplier through a dropshipping directory, don't forget to look at the supplier's in-site ratings and reviews.

2. Request for product samples. A legitimate supplier should be more than willing to provide you with samples especially if you have shown an intention of buying from them in bulk. Always request for samples if you have doubts about the quality of the products in question.

3. Attend trade shows especially those in your chosen niche or industry. This is one of the most effective ways on building and growing your business. What's great about trade shows is that you will be talking and dealing with suppliers in person unlike online wherein everyone is cloaked in anonymity.

4. Subscribe to your industry's newsletters and trade publications. There's usually a trade magazine or newsletter associated with an industry so find this trade magazine and see what you can find inside its pages. There are usually lists of suppliers, manufacturers, and traders complete with their information and contact details.

5. Join industry groups, forums, and other professional networks in your niche and industry. Networking is very important especially if your dropshipping business belongs to a very competitive niche. The connections you make will always come in handy down the road. You can get referrals or recommendations for reputable suppliers from your connections in the industry.

How to spot fake dropshipping wholesalers and suppliers:

1. They have vague contact details.

The only reason a supplier has incomplete and vague contact details is that they're covering something up. Legitimate suppliers provide several and complete contact details that may include a physical address, phone numbers, email addresses, and other basic details.

2. They refuse to provide samples.

During the negotiation process, you have every right to request for samples from the supplier. If the supplier refuses even if you are going to pay for the samples, then something is definitely wrong. A supplier who is hesitant to send samples is a huge red flag. Requesting for samples is not just a strategy to check the quality of the products, it's also a good way of verifying if the supplier is legitimate or not.

3. They sell to the public.

Be very cautious with any supplier who sells directly to the public. They are contradicting the core principle of being a dropshipping supplier when they themselves are retailing their products. Them being sellers make them direct competitors of the same entrepreneurs they are supplying.

4. They claim to provide you with very high margins.

The general rule is that if a supplier's offer is too good to be true, then it's probably not true. It's no secret that margins in the dropshipping industry are often extremely low. If someone offers you a very high margin, then something is fishy.

5. They ask for monthly membership fees.

This is not right, plain and simple. This is usually a fraudulent tactic used by scammers to deceive unsuspecting victims. There's no reason why a supplier should be charging you a monthly fee.

6. They refuse to sign contracts.

The only reason why a supplier wouldn't sign a contract is that he doesn't want to enter into a legally binding agreement. He should be more than willing to sign a contract if he's really interested in doing business with you.

Here are your options in paying for the goods you dropship from your suppliers:

1. **Credit card** – If you are just starting out, this is usually the mode of payment that most suppliers want. It's fast and convenient. It's also fairly secure. Using your credit card to order goods also allow you to rack up reward points or frequent flier miles.

2. **PayPal, Payoneer, or other online payments system** – Many suppliers prefer PayPal and other online payment systems because the transactions are often lightning-quick. The main drawback of using PayPal is that it's usually difficult to resolve an issue should something go wrong during a transaction.

3. **Net Terms on Invoice by Check or Bank Draw** – This is a very common practice in the dropshipping industry. Basically, the supplier will provide you with a certain number of days

upon which you should pay for the products you ordered. For example, let's say that you ordered goods with "net 20" terms. This means that you have 20 days to settle the purchase with your supplier either by check or bank draw.

Here are dropshipping directories where you can find suppliers and wholesalers:

- Wholesale Central - http://www.wholesalecentral.com/
- Salehoo - https://www.salehoo.com/suppliers/new
- Doba - https://www.doba.com/
- Worldwide Brands - https://www.worldwidebrands.com/
- Megagoods - https://www.megagoods.com/
- Albany Distributing - https://www.albanydistributing.com/
- Alibaba - https://www.alibaba.com/
- Oberlo - https://www.oberlo.com/
- AliDropship - https://alidropship.com/
- Dropified - https://www.dropified.com/
- Sunrise Wholesale - https://www.sunrisewholesalemerchandise.com/

Chapter Summary

Finding a good and reliable supplier or wholesaler is a crucial step in starting and growing your dropshipping business. Don't rush this step because it can come back and completely ruin your business. Never underestimate the negative effect of a bad supplier on your business. I'm not just talking about low quality products here. Low quality products from a supplier is one thing. Unreliable service from an unreliable supplier is another thing. With that said, you should only deal with a supplier who offers you two things:

1. High-quality products and
2. High quality service

If you get these two from a supplier, you are in good hands.

Did You Know

The top 10 retail eCommerce countries based on current size and future potential are, in order: USA, China, UK, Japan, Germany, France, South Korea, Russia, Belgium and Australia

Chapter 9

Managing Inventory and Multiple Suppliers

In a dropshipping business, you are not going to hold inventory but this doesn't mean there will be zero inventory management required from you. You still need inventory management skills. You have to be constantly communicating with your suppliers to make sure that orders are being fulfilled and sent on time to customers. This is sometimes referred to as indirect inventory management. In this chapter, we are going to take a quick look at how you can efficiently manage inventory and multiple suppliers.

Best Practices for Inventory Management in a Dropshipping Business

Pick products that are easier to manage.

The bigger and more fragile a product is, the more difficult it will be for you and your supplier to manage your inventories. This is why most dropshippers prefer items that are small and less likely to get damaged during transit. Have you ever wondered why so many online entrepreneurs dropship clothing? It's because clothing inventories are one of the easiest to manage. And there's the fact that clothing don't get easily damaged during shipping. In a nutshell, if you want to avoid inventory headaches, you should stick with products that are easy to store, stock, and ship.

Use multiple suppliers.

I think I've touched on this topic in an earlier chapter. Dealing with a single supplier can be disastrous to your business operations. What if that supplier suddenly runs out of stock? Or what if your only supplier keeps on delaying the shipment of product to customers? In any case, it doesn't look good for your business. The best way to fix this problem is to enter into a deal with multiple suppliers. If supplier A runs out of stock, there's supplier B or supplier C on stand by to fulfill the incoming customer orders.

Regularly check on your suppliers regarding stock availability.

In a lot of cases, inventory problems are often due to miscommunication or lack thereof. It's not always the fault of the supplier. With that said, you should make it a point to contact your suppliers every now and then to talk about product inventories. This is especially true if you are selling products that move quickly and have fast turnaround times. These are the types of products that often run out of stock.

Avoid overselling.

Overselling refers to the bad habit of accepting orders from customers even though you are not sure if your suppliers have enough inventories in stock to fulfill the orders. The general rule is that you shouldn't sell more than what your suppliers can fulfill. Overselling will hurt your business more than you think especially if it happens too often. Online consumers are a fickle bunch. Not delivering what you promised can completely turn them off. In short, overselling will lose you a lot of customers so don't do it.

Recognize that all suppliers are not alike.

If you have entered into deals with several suppliers, the quality of their services often vary. You should prioritize those who you deem to be the most reliable and most trustworthy. In the dropshipping business, nurturing relationships with your best suppliers is one of the keys to achieving success. Always think of your suppliers as long-term business partners.

Automation and technology.

You can't separate the dropshipping business model with technology tools and automation systems. These are deeply embedded together. For you to efficiently manage inventory and multiple suppliers, you have to make use of automation programs and other technological tools. You can't do everything manually and on your own. Always be on the lookout for new automation software and other digital tools that you can potentially implement on your dropshipping business.

How to Manage Multiple Dropship Suppliers

If you plan on working with multiple suppliers, you should be aware of the risks and added responsibilities that come along with it. The first rule is that you should only work with suppliers you can trust. Please refer to the chapter in this book which pertains to finding good suppliers. You have all the information you need in that chapter to find trustworthy suppliers. Now, let's say that you have entered into deals with multiple suppliers. How do you manage your responsibilities towards each supplier?

Your best bet is to make use of software that allows you to connect and communicate with several suppliers with ease. There are tons of these software out there. Find the one that's most appropriate for your business. Using automation software in managing multiple suppliers is standard practice in the dropshipping industry. It allows you to have orders fulfilled by more than one suppliers even if the orders are coming from a single customer. Trying to fulfill these orders manually will be next to impossible. With that said, my advice to you is to invest in an efficient automation software that bridges the gaps between your business and the multiple suppliers who fulfill orders from your customers.

How to Deal with Out of Stock Orders When They Occur

No matter how hard you try to ensure that your suppliers can always fulfill orders, there will be those times wherein they just can't. What do you do if this happens? The first thing you should do is contact the customer and inform him directly that the product he ordered is out of stock. If you are confident that your supplier can restock their inventory within a certain period, you can tell the customer that the product he wants will be available soon. Provide him a timeframe of when the product will be available for purchase.

If you are not sure if your supplier will be able to restock their inventory, you can try to offer the customer a similar product or even a better product. It's possible that the customer hasn't seen such a product in your listings. Inform the customer of similar products you have that have the similar features and functions of the original product he wanted. In short, don't be afraid to suggest alternatives.

Another good way to deal with out of stock orders is to outsource the orders from another supplier. In this scenario, you should find a supplier who can quickly fulfill the orders. This is not too difficult to do if you have a lot of contacts for suppliers in your niche.

Chapter Summary

For sure, managing inventory and multiple suppliers is not going to be an easy task. In fact, the complications in this sector of the business is one of the biggest reasons why a lot of new dropshippers give up. But with the right mindset and with the proper tools, you will see this as an opportunity, deal with the challenges and problems and grab more market share for yourself. It's going to be difficult at first but you will soon get used to the grind. As you gain more experience, you will be able to deal with the issues faster and with less hassle.

Did You Know

There is a huge opportunity for eCommerce growth in India – in 2014, there were 243 million internet users (19% of the population) but this is forecast to grow to 730 million users by 2020 (Sources: PwC & Nasscom and Akamai)

Chapter 10

Dealing with Security and Fraud Issues

You are running an ecommerce store which means you will always be susceptible to security and fraud issues. As your business grows and increases its profits, you will become more of a target for hackers and thieves. In this chapter, we are going to look into the best procedures on how you can protect yourself from these security and fraud issues. We are also going to talk about the solutions you can implement if your business gets actually compromised by a security and fraud problem.

How to Deal with Fraudulent Orders

A fraudulent order can be one of two things. One, it can be an unauthorized transaction by the customer. For example, a person uses another person's credit card without permission to purchase a product. Two, it could be a transaction coming from a legit source, but it was intended to defraud you. For example, a person orders a product from you, but claims that the product didn't arrive, or he claims that he didn't make the order to force you to give a refund. These fraudulent orders can result in chargebacks, which will cause you to lose a lot of money.

Here are some practical ways on how you can prevent fraudulent orders:

1. Install a built-in anti-fraud system on your dropshipping website. Again, there are a lot of software programs out there that were specifically designed to deal with fraud in businesses that follow the dropshipping model. You have many programs to choose from. You should also ask your supplier to do the same to ensure that both ends of the transactions are safe and secure.

2. Verify IP address. See to it that the IP address where the order is coming from is legit and not shady. There are also tools and software programs that allow you to automatically detect and flag down suspicious IP addresses.

3. Call the phone number associated with the order. If you will be making a big order, which means there are hundreds or even thousands of dollars involved, you should go out of your way to call the phone number and verify everything to make sure that you are fulfilling a legitimate order.

4. Search email address. Check the email address used by the customer to order from your website. Does it look suspicious? Search the email address and see if you can dig up more

information about the owner of the address. Sometimes, scammers would use bots to create fake email addresses that they then use to try and defraud ecommerce sites.

5. Check if the billing and shipping addresses match. It's often rare for a customer to use a billing address that's different from the shipping address. With that said, if the two addresses don't match, then you should treat it as a red flag. It's possible that it's an honest mistake but it's more likely that the order was fraudulent.

6. Be cautious of multiple orders with different billing addresses. If a customer places multiple orders with you but all the billing addresses are different from each other, something is definitely not right. You should check and verify with the person placing the orders. Request for an explanation why the orders have different billing addresses.

7. Review high value orders. If a customer orders thousands of dollars' worth of products from you despite the fact that you only sell products with low selling prices, something is definitely off. If a customer wants to purchase in bulk, he should be dealing with a wholesaler and not with a retailer like you. With that said, you should always review high value orders that go your way.

8. Install fraud prevention apps. There are a few dozen apps out there that can help you protect your ecommerce store from fraud and other forms of online attacks. Some of these apps have been specifically designed and developed for dropshipping businesses.

Ensuring That the Credit Card Numbers of Your Customers Are Safe and Secure

If your customers are paying you through their credit cards, it's your responsibility to ensure that their card information are always secure. Data breach can affect any online platform. Even the largest online companies are not immune to these malicious attacks. To safeguard the credit card data and other sensitive information of your customers, there are certain protocols you need to follow.

First, you should only make use of approved and tested equipment and software. The hardware and software you use should be compliant with the Payment Card Industry Data Security Standard (PCI). This applies to companies of any size that accept credit card payments from customers. If you plan on accepting card payment, then you need to host your data securely with a PCI-compliant hosting provider.

Second, don't store electronic track data or the customer's card security number in any form. This is the data contained at the black magnetic strip behind most credit cards. Track data are supposed to help merchants verify if a customer trying to purchase using the card actually has the card in his or her hands. The data also contains information that are not displayed on the surface of the card. Keep all these information secure by not copying and storing them in any form.

Third, see to it that when you store credit card account numbers, these are completely encrypted. If you are also storing the numbers in paper form, make sure that these are secured as well. Proper electronic storage of credit card numbers require a robust encryption algorithm. Even if your computer gets stolen or if someone gains access to your website, they can't just copy the credit card account numbers because these are encrypted.

Chapter Summary

Dealing with credit card security and fraud problems is serious business. Even before you launch your business, you have to review its fraud and security risks. Many hackers and credit card info thieves often target newly launched ecommerce websites because the owners are usually busy on running the business. I suggest that you get the help of a security expert to review your ecommerce website and all the software you use to make sure that every security flaw and loophole is fixed.

Did You Know

Smartphones have overtaken laptops as UK internet users' number one device, emphasising the need to have an eCommerce website that is mobile friendly to maximise sales opportunities
(Source: Ofcom)

Chapter 11

Understanding and Minimizing Chargebacks

Also often referred to as a reversal, a chargeback is a return of funds to the account of a customer. In dropshipping, the chargeback can be applied on a purchase made through a credit card or through an online payment platform like PayPal. A chargeback occurs when a customer disputes a purchase made using his or her credit card. The customer either claims that the purchase was fraudulent or the purchase was made without his knowledge or permission. During a chargeback, the credit card company reverses the transaction so that the customer is reimbursed of his money.

Needless to say, as a dropshipper, dealing with chargebacks can be a huge problem. Not only will chargebacks reduce your income, it might also cause credit card companies to penalize you if the chargebacks happen too often. When the credit card company reverses the transaction, you will usually receive an explanation for the chargeback. The reason could be any of the following: fraud, technical error, clerical error, or the customer claimed to have received a product that's inferior to what he paid for.

To reduce the number of chargebacks you deal with, here are some practical tips to help you out:

1. Get proof of shipment or delivery from delivery companies. If a customer claims non-receipt, you can always show the proof of shipment to make the point that the product made it to its destination.

2. Get in touch with the customer claiming a chargeback and verify his purchase details. Sometimes, customers forget that they've made a purchase or there's a chance that they weren't able to recognize the name of the business that appeared on their credit card statement. Have the customer recheck his transactions.

3. As much as possible, avoid manual sales processing. This is why you should make use of reliable software that automates the ordering and payment process. If you take orders manually, there's always the possibility that you make a clerical error like charging the wrong amount or charging the customer more than once.

4. Make it very easy for customers to get in touch with you. Sometimes, customers are forced to ask for a chargeback if they find it very difficult to contact and talk with you. Encourage your customers to contact you first before they start requesting for a chargeback.

5. Be responsive to customer queries. If a customer asks about a recent purchase, answer immediately. Always make it a point to respond quickly and professionally to all reasonable inquiries by your buyers.

6. Provide a crystal-clear product return policy. Make sure that your policies on refunds and returns are clear and easy to understand. If a customer doesn't know how to proceed with a possible product return because your policies are vague, he would just ask for a chargeback because it's easier to do.

7. Suggest a dispute resolution. If a customer requests for a chargeback, try resolving the issue first. Most customers are more than willing to hear suggestions on how the problem can be resolved.

Chapter Summary

As a dropshipper, you will always be dealing with chargebacks. Whether customers are paying for their purchases via credit cards or via PayPal, anyone can file for a chargeback. It's also worth mentioning here that in most cases, credit card companies and PayPal favor customers by default unless you can provide undeniable proof that the problem causing the chargeback was not your fault. You can lessen your chargeback problems by following the practical tips I've discussed above.

Did You Know

Clothes and sports goods are the most popular categories from which people buy online from in the UK (Source: Statista)

Chapter 12

Dealing With Product Returns and Shipping Issues

Product returns and shipping issues are a huge source of headaches in dropshipping. This is why it's very important that you come up with a comprehensive return policy. Such a policy should cover all instances of returns due to damaged goods, destroyed goods in transit, defective goods, and goods returned for the simple reason that the customer wasn't satisfied with it. Setting up a return policy in a dropshipping business is further complicated by the fact that you aren't the one shipping the products. But this shouldn't intimidate you. Dealing with product returns doesn't have to be that difficult. In this chapter, I'm going to show you how you can make it easier for you.

When Does a Return Happen?

A product return happens when a customer who previously bought an item from you wants to return the product and requests for a refund or a replacement. There are various reasons why a customer would return a product. These include the following: incorrect product, incorrect size, product no longer needed, product does not match the description, product did not meet customer's expectations, and deliberate fraud. With regards to how to deal with deliberate fraud, please refer to Chapter 10 and Chapter 11.

If a buyer wants to return a product, the process looks like this:
1. A customer gets in touch with you and asks for a return
2. You contact your supplier who fulfilled the order and ask for an RMA (return merchandise authorization)
3. The customer ships back the product to your supplier. The RMA number should be highlighted on the shipping address.
4. After receiving the product, your supplier refunds you the cost of the product.
5. After getting your refund, you in turn send a refund to the customer for the amount he paid for the returned product.

However, the process is not always this simple. Complications can arise due to defective products and restocking fees. A restocking fee is basically a surcharge for the products returned by your customers. It's best that when you write your return policy, don't make your customers pay for the restocking fees. You should handle the restocking fees yourself.

When it comes to defective items returned by customers, it's bad business practice to have the customer pay for the fees associated with shipping the product back to the supplier. Again, you should handle the fees. It's part of the costs of running an online dropshipping business. When writing your return policy, make sure that you make it clear that you will be handling the postage and shipping fees for products that are returned due to defects. It's simply not right to make a customer suffer and then let him incur further expenses when shipping the defective product back to your supplier. Taking care of this also gives the customer confidence and will increase the chance of him/her buying from you.

Dealing with Shipping Issues

When pricing the products you list on your dropshipping website, you should take into account your shipping costs. Calculating these can be challenging especially if you are working with several suppliers who are in different locations. It can be difficult to accurately calculate the shipping rates for different orders. When calculating the rates, you can use the following methods:

1. **Real-Time Rates** – You calculate the shipping rates by taking into account the destination of the shipment and the collective weight of all the products purchased. This method provides you with an actual real-time price quote. It's an accurate method but it becomes problematic if customer orders are being fulfilled by several suppliers from different locations.

2. **Per-Type Rates** – With this method, you assign flat shipping rates to products based on their types or categories. Let's say you are selling two types of a product (Type A and Type B). Type A products will be shipped for a flat rate of $15 while Type B products will ship for a flat rate of $30. Needless to say, this is a much simpler method but the shipping rates aren't as accurate compared to real-time rates.

3. **Flat-Rate Shipping** – This is the simplest method for the simple reason that you charge a single flat rate for all your products regardless of their type or category. It's the simplest but it's also the least accurate. Never use this method if you are selling a lot of products whose prices vary widely.

International Shipments

If you plan on selling your products to an international market, there are several factors you must take into account when it comes to shipping costs. One, shipping rates aren't always similar for different countries. Some charge much more and some charge much less. Two, most suppliers will request for an additional fee from you for processing international orders. This is understandable because processing international orders requires more work. Three, shipping heavy and large products internationally can be very costly. My advice is that you should avoid selling heavy and bulky products internationally. And last but not the least, you should take into account the fact that it's often difficult to resolve shipping problems associated with international orders. You will not only be dealing with shipping issues in one country, you are dealing with shipping issues concerning two countries.

Chapter Summary

Before you launch your dropshipping business, make sure that you have a complete and clear return policy in order. The policy should discuss in detail how customers can return products and how they can request for refunds. Don't make the mistake of writing a vague return policy because this will only confuse your customers. When writing the policy, you should also take into account the types of products you are selling and the countries you are shipping them to.

Likewise, you should also try to understand all the issues associated with shipping your products. What are the costs of shipping your products? How should you compute these shipping costs? Based on your computations, is it worth it shipping your products internationally? These are just some of the important questions you should ask yourself with regards to the shipping aspect of your ecommerce business. Again, if you are not yet sure on how to proceed, I highly recommend that you consult with someone who has the proper knowledge and experience about dropshipping returns and shipping issues.

Did You Know

Because of forced account registration, online users abandon their shopping carts 26% of the time. Shopping cart abandonment accounts for $18 billion in lost revenue each year!

Chapter 13

10 Beginner Mistakes and How to Avoid Them

Learn from the mistakes of those who went ahead of you. This will be the mantra for this chapter. If you are inexperienced, it's expected that you are going to make mistakes along the way. That is normal and it happens to everyone. In this chapter, we are going to look at the most common mistakes that beginners make when they start and build a dropshipping business for the first time. Being aware of these common mistakes would help you in avoiding them.

1. Selling a lot of products right off the bat.

Dropshipping a single product in itself is very hard. What more if you are selling several products. I am not saying that selling a lot of products is bad. I'm saying that you shouldn't do it if you are just starting out. You're not building a general store wherein you need to sell a lot of products. It's very difficult to carve your own market in the industry if you are selling too many products. Selling niche products is still your best chance of attracting a good number of recurring customers online because you'll be able to fully understand the customer requirements in that niche i.e. your customer avatar

2. Not checking the background and experience of a supplier or manufacturer.

Newbie dropshippers often focus on cheap products and low shipping costs that they fail to verify if the supplier is reliable or not. I say it again, your business is just as good as your supplier. If you have a bad supplier, it follows that your business is going to be bad. This is why you should only deal with suppliers and manufacturers whose reputation can be verified online via reviews and referrals. Never enter into a deal with a supplier whose background and experience you know nothing about.

3. Not requesting for samples of the products to be dropshipped.

It may be hard to believe but a lot of new ecommerce entrepreneurs make this completely avoidable mistake. Not requesting for samples of the product is a recipe for disaster. Getting samples is the only way for you to know if the products are up to your standards. You have to check if the products look and function the way the supplier advertised them. If a supplier refuses to send you samples, then something is amiss. If the supplier truly wants to do business with you, he should be more than willing to send you product samples. Sending you the samples shouldn't be a problem because in most cases, you are going to pay for the samples yourself.

4. Not getting your finances in order.

Many newbies often make the rookie mistake of building a business financially blind. That is they are clueless with regards to how much they need to get started and where they are going to get the funds. They start ordering products without assessing what their profit margins (i.e. net profit as a percentage of revenue) will be. They start dealing with suppliers without determining if their prices are too high or too low. The best way to get your finances in order is to get the services of an accountant, a business consultant, or any related professional who can help you get a clear understanding of your expenses, costs, and projected earnings.

5. Relying too much on vendors.

Putting too much trust in a vendor is seldom a good strategy. This is something you should be wary of especially if you are dropshipping products from a one or two vendors. You have to ask the question: what if the vendor suddenly bails out on you? Your business will done because there's no source for products. You need to start all over again from scratch. To avoid this problem, what you should do is deal only with vendors who have verifiable track records. For insurance purposes, you should draw out a contract which you and the vendor agree to. Last but not the least, try dealing with several vendors, not just one vendor.

6. Expecting to make instant money.

Many people have the wrong assumption that dropshipping is a get-rich-quick operation. Nope, it's not. Although there are those who get lucky and make a ton of cash from the get-go but for most starters, it's a long road towards profits and success. Don't be greedy. Don't believe in the lofty claims of those who are saying that you can be rich overnight with dropshipping. To reach that point, you have to work hard and work smart. Start the business with realistic goals and expectations.

7. Selling trademarked products.

You cannot sell products that are registered copyrights or registered trademarks of another company. You can only sell them if you have asked permission from them and they obliged. In most cases, you are required to get a license before you are able to sell them. You should also be careful about the suppliers and manufacturers where you are sourcing your products. See to it that they are not using trademark-protected elements like logos, images, and designs. To avoid getting entangled in trademark and copyright issues, you should focus on selling white-label products. What's great about white-label products is that you can customize their logos and designs to make them your own. You can run a quick trademark search at the <u>United States Patent and</u> <u>Trademark Office</u> website.

8. Giving up too soon.

This is one of the biggest reasons why most people who try dropshipping never reach their full potential. How can they reach their goals when they gave up at the first sign of trouble? As I kept saying in earlier chapters, you are going to face a lot of problems and challenges along the way especially in the early stages of your business. These failures, big and small, can be very discouraging. But you should not let them break you down and cause you to give up. Just keep going. Learn from your mistakes and make sure that you don't make them again.

9. Unreliable customer support.

A lot of newbie dropshippers often take customer support for granted. They sometimes assume that this part of the business is handled by the shipping party. Often unprepared, they are clueless as to what to do when they are inundated by complaints and shipping problems. Customers, especially online shoppers, get easily pissed off by bad and unreliable customer service. Bad customer service will prevent you from growing your business. In short, you need to invest in a reliable customer service system.

10. Picking the wrong niche.

Beginners often stumble when it comes to choosing the right niche for their dropshipping business. They often go chasing lucrative but very competitive niches. Another common mistake by beginners is that they get into a niche where they have very little knowledge about. This is problematic for two main reasons. One, it will be very difficult for you to answer questions and inquiries by customers. And two, your competitors are more knowledgeable about the products than you and this will reflect in how they present their unique value proposition. So who will the customers most likely to support? You who know very little about the products? Or your competitors who present their products in a way that appeals to the customer in addition to having all the answers to every customer inquiry?

Chapter Summary

The bottom line here is that it's okay to make mistakes and make the wrong decisions early on in the business. It would be unrealistic to expect the business to be sailing smoothly without encountering any problems. What you can do is either try to avoid making these mistakes or prepare for them. The common mistakes we have discussed in this chapter should be more than enough to help you prepare and anticipate. Go over the list a few more times before you start working on your dropshipping business. Understanding these mistakes can save you a lot of money, time, and resources down the road.

Did You Know

A single second delay in your website loading time can result in a 7% loss in conversion, and 40% of web users will abandon a website if it takes longer than 3 seconds to load.

Chapter 14

How To Scale Your Dropshipping Business

Scaling a business is never easy. People often make the assumption that scaling a business is just a matter of adding products to your inventory or doubling your operations. In reality, it's not as simple as that. Selling five products instead of two products doesn't automatically scale the business. There are so many other factors that determine if the business is being scaled or otherwise. In this chapter, we are going to discuss some of the best strategies on how to actually grow and scale your business.

Here are 7 powerful strategies you can use to scale up your business:

1. Add value to your products.

What is meant by adding value to your products? It means improving the product so that a customer will purchase it from you instead of purchasing it from a competitor. Needless to say, adding value to a product is very important if you are promoting products that are very similar to what other entrepreneurs are selling. You need to add value to your products to make them unique in the eyes of consumers. But how exactly do you accomplish this? Well, you have a lot of options.

There are several ways to add value to your products. One, you can customize their designs and packaging so they look more enticing to customers. Two, you can offer accessories on top of your main products. Three, you can create a loyalty program wherein customers get significant discounts the more they buy from you. You may not know it but offering a lower price is actually a form of adding value to your products. Four, you can also offer discounts for bulk purchases. For example, if a customer buys ten units, he will get one unit free. That one free unit is considered as added value by the customer.

Last but not the least, just make your products better than everybody else's. The better you make your products, the more valuable they are in the eyes of your target customers. Better products also translates into more sales. More sales means your business is being scaled to higher heights.

2. Focus a lot of your attention on marketing and search engine optimization (SEO).

In many ways, scaling a business is synonymous to ramping up your marketing campaigns. That means if you want to scale your dropshipping business, you have to double or triple your marketing efforts. The harder you promote a product, the more customers you attract and the more sales you make. That's scaling in its purest form. Now, there are many strategies on how to promote a product online but you should focus most of your attention on just a few ones. These strategies are as follows:

- ✓ **Search engine optimization** - Organic traffic or traffic coming from search engines is the best type of online traffic. These are people who are specifically looking for your product. This means that they are more than likely to purchase the product from you. Organic traffic is much easier to convert into paying customers compared to other types of traffic because they know what they want and they know your product will help them satisfy their need. Now, the only way for you to get organic traffic is through search engine optimization or SEO. You have to optimize your dropshipping website with the proper keyword combinations for it to be able to attract traffic from Google.

- ✓ **Social media marketing** – Social media traffic is starting to catch up with the level of traffic that Google has. In fact, next to Google, the most visited websites in the world are social media sites (i.e. Facebook, Twitter, Instagram, and YouTube). With that said, it would be a huge mistake if you aren't active in promoting your products and dropshipping business on social media platforms. Most social sites are free to use so there's absolutely no reason why you shouldn't leverage them to your advantage.

- ✓ **Content marketing** – This is a rather broad term but it's basically about creating online content that's designed to promote and drive traffic to your dropshipping website. Forms of content marketing include blogging, guest writing, article marketing, sponsoring posts, and press releases. For example, you write an article and distribute it to bloggers if they are interested in publishing it. It's up to you if you decide to pay them or not. They publish the article on their blogs. The article would contain a mention of your business and a link to your website. This is content marketing in its purest form.

- ✓ **Advertising** – To make money, you have to spend money. This is especially true today wherein the competition among online entrepreneurs is getting tougher by the day. Sometimes, the only way to get ahead of your competitors is to be aggressive with your advertising campaigns. Fortunately, you have many options when it comes to advertising online. You can make use of advertising programs like Google Adsense or you can directly advertise in websites and blogs you specifically choose. You should also consider purchasing ads in popular social media sites.

3. Leveraging Facebook ads to drive traffic to your dropshipping website.

Facebook is the perfect platform to promote your dropshipping business. The social networking site has more than a billion active users and it's growing by the thousands every single day. This is a huge market you can tap into. The best way to promote your business on Facebook is to take advantage of its advertising program. It's very cheap, it's very easy to use, and most importantly, it gets good results.

Getting Started with Facebook Ads

➢ All you need to get started is a Facebook account and a Facebook page for your business.

➢ You have several options on how to promote something on Facebook. You can purchase an ad for the page itself, an ad for a specific post in your page, or an ad that promotes a link which directs to your main dropshipping website.

➢ The first time you purchase an ad, you will be required to add a payment method to your account. You can use a credit card, a bank account, or PayPal. Facebook will charge you through any of these payment methods every time an ad campaign of yours is completed.

Advantages of Using Facebook Ads for Your Dropshipping Business

- It's very cheap. You can purchase an ad and have it run for a whole day and pay just a few dollars for it. You can attract thousands of eyeballs from that one ad alone depending on how effective your targeting is. A well crafted customer avatar makes a huge difference.

- You can pause and cancel an ad any time you like. If you realize that the ad isn't getting the number of clicks you expected, you can always pause it so that you can optimize it for a better performance. Alternatively, you can cancel the ad altogether. You will only pay for the period during which the ad has been live.

- You only pay for the ads after the campaign. For example, you purchased an ad for one week and you set a budget of $200. You will only be billed at the end of one week.

- Facebook ads allow you to narrow down your target audience. You can customize an ad by geographical location, age range, gender, and interests. You literally specify the types of Facebook users who will be able to see your ads. This is perfect if your dropshipping business caters to a small and specific niche.

- Facebook provides you with data and statistics about the performances of your ads. You can determine how many clicks, views, likes, and shares your ads are getting. In short, you can better analyse if your target customers are engaging with your ads or not.

Disadvantages of Using Facebook Ads for Your Dropshipping Business

- Sometimes, you get very low engagement because most people use Facebook to be entertained and not to look for products. Ads on the site are often treated as nuisance by a lot of users.

- It costs money. Although advertising on Facebook is cheap, it can still be an issue especially if you have a very tight budget.

Its fair to say the advantages significantly outnumber the disadvantages. Facebook is a tool that you should be using to advertise and scale your business. The social site's advertising program has quite a number of flaws but these are trivial compared to the immense benefits you can get from taking advantage of the program. If you're interested in learning, step-by-step, how to fully take advantage of the Facebook advertising platform to scale your business, I invite you to take a look at my book – Facebook Advertising Made Easy.

4. Specialize or niche down your products.

This refers to the strategy of increasing your products by further dividing your niche into categories. In short, you niche down your products. For example, let's say that you are selling running shoes on your dropshipping website. You can niche them down by creating categories like trail running shoes and road running shoes. Trail running shoes are designed for rugged, rough, and uneven trails while road running shoes are designed for even pavements and roads. You are niching down while increasing the number of products you are selling. You can further divide the categories based on metrics like brand or even the materials used to manufacture them.

5. Automate your store.

In automating your dropshipping business, you are not only making it easier for your customers and your team, you are also freeing up a lot of time and resources which you can then further invest in growing the business. In automating the business, you are hitting two birds with one stone. Automation also allows you to add more products to your listings without increasing the burden of running the business.

6. Private label or retail arbitrage.

How retail arbitrage works is quite simple. You look for products in an online marketplace like Amazon or eBay or AliExpress then list these in your own online store. If a customer purchases a product from your website, you order the product from the online marketplace where you found it. The original source of the product processes and fulfills the order. You earn from the difference between your selling price and the original source's price. You can scale your dropshipping business by engaging in this sales model.

On the other hand, private labeling refers to the business practice of rebranding products by another company and selling these as if they are your own. For example, let's say you enter into a deal with a private label company to produce a line of beauty products for you. These are usually generic beauty products. You customize them and make them your own by putting your own designs, logos, and choice of packaging on them. You can make a deal so that the supplier also handles shipping of the products to your customers. You receive the orders from customers then forward these to your supplier.

7. Offer outstanding service.

How you deal with your customers plays a very important role in the growth of your business. Scaling your business will be very difficult if your core customers are not satisfied with your services. Good service nurtures loyalty among your customers. Good service is a driver of growth. Let me put it this way. A customer buys a product from you and because you delivered a high-quality product on time and at the right price, that customer will likely buy from you again or even spread the good word about your business to their friends and family via word of mouth. And just like that you've potentially doubled or tripled your business because of that one customer. Just imagine if most of your new customers turn into repeat customers. You will be scaling your business in no time.

Chapter Summary

As you can see, scaling a dropshipping business takes a lot of work and time. There's a long road ahead of you so you need to work harder, and most importantly, smarter. When setting your scaling goals, make them long-term and set clear actions steps you can take to achieve them. This way you won't overwhelm yourself. With that said, don't be too hard on yourself. That's one of the keys in ensuring that you always have the right mindset and that you are always on the right track. If you implement all the scaling strategies I have discussed above, you will be well on your way to achieving sustained success. At the end of the day, that's what matters. As long as you are doing things right, growth will come sooner or later.

Did You Know

Amazon is king of the ecommerce jungle. Speaking of not having a close second. Amazon brought in $79.2 billion in sales in 2015. The next closest online retailer is wal-mart.com which brought in $13.4 billion. Following suit are Apple with $12 billion and staples.com with $10 billion. It doesn't seem like a fair contest, does it?

Other Notable Books By Michael Ezeanaka	
Book #	**Book Title**
1	Affiliate Marketing Made Easy
2	55 Passive Income Ideas Analysed
3	Amazon FBA Mastery
4	Dropshipping
5	Real Estate Investing For Beginners
6	Credit Card Mastery
7	Facebook Advertising Made Easy
8	Stock Market Investing For Beginners
The kindle edition will be available to you for FREE when you purchase the paperback version from Amazon.com (The US Store)	

Chapter 15

15 Practical Tips and Lessons From Successful Dropshippers

This chapter is what I call the Inspiration Chapter. It's always a good idea to watch what successful dropshippers are doing and listen to what they have to say. If you want to make money from dropshipping, then you should learn from those who have already done it. I wrote this chapter to provide you with inspiration and the added drive to be successful in this industry. So let's dig in:

1. Don't be greedy.

Greediness is a nasty attribute that has no place in the dropshipping business. If your plan is to make as much money as you can in the shortest time possible, then you are in the wrong business. It's more likely that your business will crash and burn, and leave you with irredeemable costs. Dropshipping is not a get-rich-quick scheme. Most of the successful dropshippers you see out there didn't get to where they are by being greedy and aggressive. They built their dropshipping businesses through hard work and smart decisions. These are the same things you need to start and build your own successful dropshipping business.

2. Focus on evergreen products.

What is an evergreen product? In the simplest of terms, an evergreen product is a product that is still in demand regardless of the time of year. It's the very opposite of a seasonal product. T-shirts are evergreen products. Christmas sweaters are seasonal products. Jackets are evergreen products. Halloween costumes are seasonal products. I am not in any way saying that you should completely ignore seasonal products. You can still build a successful dropshipping business selling seasonal products, but if you want to create a business that's sustainable and profitable *all year round*, then your focus should be on evergreen products.

3. Find a niche that's connected to something you are passionate about.

In our example, if you love and enjoy trail running, then it makes complete sense to start a dropshipping business that sells all sorts of products related to trail running. These may include trail running shoes, accessories, hiking sandals, running shorts, etc. The biggest benefit of building a business around a hobby or interest is that there's little chances of you burning yourself out. Why should you burn yourself out when you enjoy what you are doing most of the time? The more you love the niche, the more you will enjoy running the business. Work becomes play. That's something that a lot of aspiring entrepreneurs dream about.

4. Constantly find ways on how to automate aspects of your business.

There are so many tools and resources out there that enable you to automate your dropshipping business. Many of these tools are even free to use. Automation is very important especially if you can't focus your whole attention on running the business. Automation also helps in growing and scaling your business quickly. Some of the things you can automate include marketing tasks, advertising tasks, emails, ad retargeting, and even customer service. Simplifying and automating the tasks associated with managing a dropshipping business have never been easier. You just have to find the right tools, plugins, and add-ons.

5. Invest in a good website design and theme.

Here's something you should know about online consumers. They often judge ecommerce stores based on their designs. If your dropshipping store has a bad design, people will likely think that you have bad products as well. Badly designed websites are less trustworthy in the eyes of online consumers. With that said, you should invest in a good website designer who can create for you a simple but professional-looking ecommerce store. It's not that difficult to find an experienced developer these days considering the proliferation of freelancers. It's best that you hire a developer who mostly works in building dropshipping-related websites. Freelancers can be found on sites like Upwork and Fiverr.

6. Offer Exceptional Customer Service

Customers may not always remember the product they bought from your website but they will always remember how you treated them. Customer service is very important in the dropshipping business considering the fact that you are not handling the products yourself. Somebody else is shipping the products to your customers so there's a higher risk of product returns and complaints. If your business receives a lot of orders in a day, I highly recommend that you provide customer service on a 24/7 basis. Hire two customer service representatives. One will work in the morning and one will work at night. Offering exceptional customer service is one of the most effective ways in building loyalty among your customers.

7. Request for Product Samples Before You Start Shipping Them to Customers

Don't rely on the words of your supplier or manufacturer. The general rule is that before you even list a product on your ecommerce store, make sure that you have thoroughly checked a sample of the product. There's no other way around this. You have to check the product first before you start selling it. Instruct your supplier to send you a batch of the products so that you can check several of the items. Don't assume that the products look exactly how they were advertised.

Requesting for product samples offers several benefits. These include the following:

- It offers you the chance to experience what it is like to buy a product from you. This allows you to identify issues with the process and come up with possible solutions.
- You can use the sample products for online advertisements, review videos, and other promotional materials.
- Being able to touch and look at the physical product helps you in coming up with a better and more detailed product description.
- The samples help you in getting better quality photos of your products.

8. Only work with a supplier who has extensive experience in the business.

When browsing through a dropshipping directory, you are going to come across thousands of dropshippers. Most of them have very little experience in the business. It would be a mistake if you are going to anchor your business on an inexperienced supplier. It's easy to spot inexperienced suppliers in a dropshipping directory. One, they usually have zero or very few reviews and comments. And two, their prices and costs tend to be much lower than average. Suppliers with extensive experience in the industry are often much more expensive but you are better off dealing with them. At least you are assured of the quality of their products and services. Dealing with inexperienced suppliers is just too risky especially if it's your first time to start and build an ecommerce store.

9. Look for light and durable products instead of heavy and fragile products.

When it comes to deciding which products to sell through dropshipping, it's very tempting to decide on items that have a lot of suppliers around. But before you start thinking of selling products like home theatre systems, porcelain vases, and other profitable but fragile products, remind yourself of how risky these products are. Selling fragile products is a recipe for disaster. Before you know it, you are dealing with countless product returns and chargebacks. Logistics is among your most important concerns when shipping products. It is always better to consider light and durable products instead of heavy and fragile items. They are easier and much cheaper to ship.

10. Sell Products That You Know

It's always a safe choice to promote and sell products that you are knowledgeable about. Having the right knowledge about the products you are selling means you will be able to take out the guesswork out of your choice of products. Your knowledge and expertise about the items you are selling will show in the level of customer service you can provide, in your confidence in the deals you offer, and in the way you present your products in your ecommerce website. Another important benefit of selling products that you know is that it will significantly improve your ratings as a seller. Seller ratings are a major driving force in dropshipping. It helps in improving the confidence that customers have towards you and your products.

11. Consider paying extra for tracking numbers and shipping insurance.

In dropshipping, there is always the risk that a customer's package gets damaged or lost. It would be very difficult to try and retrieve the lost products if you don't have a shipping insurance or if you don't have a system for tracking numbers. There are two major problems you can face if you don't have tracking numbers and shipping insurance. One, you can lose a lot of money from lost packages. And two, you will get a lot of negative and unflattering reviews and feedback from your customers. With that said, I suggest that you consider paying extra cash for tracking numbers and shipping insurance.

12. Be ready for product returns, back orders, and lost packages.

These are the biggest problems in a business with a dropshipping model. Never forget the fact that you do not have direct control over the handling and shipping of your products to the end customers. You have to plan properly and prepare for these contingencies. Your best strategy is to discuss policies about these returns and back orders with your suppliers. It should be clear who is going to handle these problems. Discuss the responsibilities and obligations of all parties involved (you as the business owner and the supplier as your dropshipper). This ensures that all parties exert their best efforts in avoiding product returns, back orders, and lost packages.

13. Use a reliable order management and dropshipping system.

There should be a reliable and secure connection between your business and your supplier. Getting the system to work properly can be difficult especially if you are dealing with more than one suppliers. Working with more than one suppliers means you have to set up more than one system connections. It's also worth mentioning here that some suppliers also deal with several ecommerce website owners. This means that they are also managing several accounts and this can further complicate the process. There are many platforms that you can use to make this simpler. Again, you should take your time in weighing your options. Some of the more well-known order management systems today include Orderhive, Ordoro, and Sellbrite.

14. A high quality presentation of your products should be among your top priorities.

Here is something you should understand about online shoppers. They often judge products based on how these look on their browsers and devices. If the photo of a product you have listed in your ecommerce website is blurry and amateurish, it would be very hard for a customer to take it seriously. Needless to say, you should invest in a good camera that allows you to take clear, crisp and professional-looking photos of your products. Also learn image-manipulation skills so that you can further improve the presentation of your products. If you don't have time for all these, try hiring a professional product photographer or a graphics designer. Presentation plays a very important role in ecommerce. If people visit your website and they see bad product photos, they'll likely click to leave.

15. Try building a brand around your dropshipping business.

Branding is very important in online sales. Consumers tend to support businesses that they can easily recall or relate with. Branding is not just about putting your products in as many platforms as possible. It's also about maintaining a set of products that have the same feel, look, and quality. Your business should have a strong voice. The brand you are going to create around your business should be catered towards your target market. For example, if you are targeting teens and young adults, the look, feel, and language you use in your website should be relatable to teens and young adults.

Chapter Summary

In the dropshipping industry, watching and learning is one of the best ways to steer your business to success. Watch what successful dropshippers are doing and try to model them. Look at the most successful entrepreneurs in your niche and watch closely what they are doing. How are they presenting their products online? How are they marketing their products? What kinds of software are they using? Where are they getting their suppliers? How are they running their customer support systems? How are they dealing with product returns? All these questions have been answered in this chapter. Try rereading the chapter to fully understand the great importance of every single tip and advice discussed herein.

Did You Know

Asia is the largest online purchasing group. As large and staggering as US online sales are, Asia claims close to 37% of online sales volume. To be clear, this includes China, South Korea and Japan. On a related note, the UK can claim close to 27% of web-based revenue.

Chapter 16

How to Promote Your Dropshipping Business

I don't have to tell you that the competition online is as tough as it gets. This is especially true if you decide to enter a popular market where there are literally thousands of online stores selling the same products. The thing about online competition is that it's going to get even tougher in the coming months and years as more entrepreneurs try their luck with ecommerce. This is something you should be aware of by now. With that said, you have to do everything to get ahead of the competition. Aside from offering high-quality products at very affordable prices, another proven method of getting ahead of the competition is to market your business like crazy.

Marketing is the key to being successful online especially in the dropshipping business. You have to devote a lot of your time and resources in telling people about your products and how good these products are. You should take a page from Coca-Cola's marketing strategy. Do you know why Coca-Cola is the biggest soda seller for decades? It's because they have mastered the art of marketing their products to every single platform available. Everywhere you look, there's a Coca-Cola logo or advertisement. It has come to the point wherein if you think about soda, Coca-Cola always comes to mind.

Applying the same marketing concept, you should try to promote your products and business in as many platforms as possible. Put your products out there where more people will get to see them. Since you are running an online dropshipping business, nearly all of your marketing efforts will be concentrated online. What's great about online marketing is that you are on an even field with the big companies. You may not have the same marketing budget as them but you have the chance of reaching millions of potential customers with the right marketing strategy.

Alright, without further ado, let's now take a look at some of the most effective marketing strategies that you can use to promote your business and products online. These are very practical strategies that can be easily implemented so there's absolutely no reason why you shouldn't apply them. You don't have to do all of them especially if you are too busy doing other things. But you should at least try them whenever you get the chance.

1. Content Marketing

How content marketing works is pretty simple and straightforward. You create content which can be in the form of articles, images, infographics, videos, or a combination of all of these types of digital content. You then distribute this content to as many platforms as you can. For example, you can write a long and detailed article then send it to media outlets, press release portals, blogs, websites, and forums. Those who want to publish the article can publish it. So how does this benefit you and your business? It's simple. The content you distribute mentions you and your business or it contains a link that redirects to your own website.

In a way, content marketing accomplishes two important things. One, it helps in spreading the word about you, your business, your brand, and your products. Imagine if a major news outlet like the New York Times publishes your article. This is a major boost to your business and brand. The second important thing that content marketing accomplishes is traffic generation. Content marketing is very good in driving web traffic to your website. And we're not just talking about ordinary traffic here. We are talking about traffic that's genuinely interested in what you are offering.

How good is content marketing in generating traffic to your website? Again, imagine if an article you wrote gets published in the New York Times. This is a major media outlet that generates millions of hits a day. That single article can drive hundreds of thousands of new visitors to your website if it gets traction on the New York Times website. The traffic can be in the millions if the article goes viral. Of course, this is just an example and the chance of getting published in the New York Times is small at best but you get the idea. Content marketing is a very powerful traffic generation strategy. Even if you are targeting smaller platforms like blogs and forums, the new traffic you get is just as valuable.

2. Social Media Marketing

If you are not using social media to market your business and products, then you are missing out on a lot of sales and opportunities. Ignoring the power of social media is akin to shooting yourself in the foot. You may be ignoring the social platforms but you are hurting yourself and your business in the process. If you are not already leveraging social media, now is the time to get on the bandwagon. Social media is the future of online marketing. This is not an exaggeration.

Just come to think of it. The largest and most influential online companies today are social media sites. There's Facebook, YouTube, Instagram, Twitter, WhatsApp, and Snapchat, just to name a few. These are the most visited websites on the internet today. The only online platform that beats them when it comes to organic traffic is Google, which is a search engine. But if you look at the data and trends, more and more people are moving away from search engines and towards social media sites. They get their news and entertainment from social sites. They get news updates from Facebook. They entertain themselves on YouTube or Instagram. The direction of the trends are pretty simple. More people are getting involved in social media. And it would be tragic to your business if you don't take advantage of this phenomenon.

Social media marketing is not that difficult to do. Of course, your marketing strategy should be tailored depending on the social media site that you are using. Marketing on Facebook is very different from marketing on YouTube. There are tons of tools and resources online that will teach you exactly how you can promote products on specific social media sites. You should take advantage of these resources whenever you can.

3. Search Engine Optimization (SEO)

I'm sure that you have heard of search engine optimization one too many times. You're probably sick and tired of hearing about it. But that doesn't take away the fact that SEO is one of the most powerful ways on how to market something online. The goal of optimization is very simple. And that is to improve the rankings of your website on Google's search results. If you run a dropshipping business that sells customized soccer balls, then you would like your website to appear at the top of the search results when someone types the phrase "customized soccer balls".

To be able to conduct SEO properly, you need to understand how Google ranks websites in the search results. There are several factors that the search engine takes into account when deciding how a website ranks. These factors include the quality of the content of the website, the age of the website, the number of links that point to the website, the social media chatter around the website, and the relevance of the website's content to the searcher's query. Needless to say, if you want to optimize your website, you need to address most if not all of these factors.

To start with the optimization process, you need to find out about the words, terms, and phrases that people use to look for your products. These are commonly referred to as keywords. In your perspective as a dropshipper, there are two main types of keywords. There are the keywords that people are currently using to arrive at your website. And then there are the keywords that you want people to use to arrive at your website. There's a big difference between the two. The first one consists of keywords that you are already ranking for. The second consists of keywords that you want to rank for.

Keyword research is the best way to look for the keywords that are most relevant to your business and products. There are several keyword research tools that you can use but I highly recommend that you use Google's own keyword tool. It's free and it offers the most accurate data on keywords. All you need is a Gmail account to access the tool. With the tool, you can determine how many people are searching for specific keywords on a monthly basis. This allows you to decide whether it's worth it to target a keyword or not.

After doing your keyword research, you should have in your hands a comprehensive list of words, terms, and phrases that people would use to search for your products. The next step is to create content that integrates these words and phrases. However, you need to be careful when writing keyword-optimized content. Don't overdo it or your website will be tagged for keyword stuffing. This refers to the unethical practice of putting too many keywords in an article in an attempt to game Google's algorithm. This strategy is against Google's quality requirements. If you are caught doing it, Google can penalize you by demoting your website in the search rankings. If you break the rule one too many times, Google might go as far as banning your site altogether. Needless to say, keyword stuffing is something you should never even think of doing.

4. Direct Advertising

The term direct advertising is a loose term but it allow me to offer a basic definition and interpretation in the context of the dropshipping business model. As the term implies, what you do is directly get in touch with the owners of websites, blogs, or social media pages where you want to advertise your website. For example, let's say that you run a dropshipping business selling soccer shoes. What you need to do is approach webmasters and owners of websites, blogs, and social sites that are relevant to the sport of soccer. The readers of these websites are soccer fans so it makes sense that you are going to purchase direct advertising from them.

One of the biggest benefits of direct advertising is that you can negotiate for the prices you want. This is different compared to other online advertising programs wherein you don't have control over the advertising prices. You are directly dealing with the website owners. This gives you more room in the negotiation table.

To be successful in direct advertising, you have to learn the tricks of the sales pitch. The sales pitch is your ticket to getting a good deal with a website owner or manager. In writing the sales pitch, you have to convince the website owner that your business is a good fit for the website. That you are offering products which the readers of the website will likely be interested in. You have to explain that not only are you paying the website owner for the advertising space, you are also offering value to the website's readers. With a good sales pitch, it shouldn't be that hard to find websites that will enter into an advertising deal with you.

To help you get the most out of your direct advertising efforts, here are some practical tips you can follow:

- Make your sales pitch as simple as possible. This is especially true if you are targeting a fairly popular blog or website. If you are sending the message via email, make it just a few paragraphs. Simply tell the website owner what your website is all about and why you would like to rent advertising space from him. Make sure to add some information as to why your business would be a good fit for the website's readers. Don't beat around the bush. Just go straight to the point.

- Be very clear about the types and sizes of ads that you want to display on the website. You should understand that ads are priced based on their sizes and where they are displayed on the website. The bigger the ad, the more expensive it becomes. If a website owner is interested in taking you in as an advertiser, that's when you start talking about ad sizes and ad locations.

- Make use of attention-grabbing headlines. This is one of the most effective strategies in online marketing. You have to create headlines that immediately grab the attention of readers. Again, you have to make it short and simple because most of the time you are working with very limited space. There's just not much that you can fit in a 300x300 advertisement, for example.

- Make use of call-to-action buttons. What are call-to-action buttons? These are the digital signifiers that instruct people to do something or follow up on something. For example, you come across an advertisement in a website that says "Click here", "Call now!" or "Subscribe now!". These are call-to-action buttons. They are effective in the sense that people tend to do things when they are reminded to do them. An advertisement that contains a "Buy now" call-to-action button performs better and generates more sales compared to an advertisement that contains no call-to-action buttons.

- Use a combination of textual, image-based, and video-based advertisements. It would be a mistake to focus on a single type of advertisement. It's not that difficult to create image-based and video-based ads these days. There are so many online tools and resources that you can use to create these types of ads. Textual advertisements are perfect for content-heavy websites. Image-based and video-based advertisements, on the other hand, tend to perform better when shown in image and video sites.

- Follow up on your sales pitches. Just because a person you messaged earlier doesn't respond to your proposal doesn't necessarily mean that he's not interested in your advertising offer. It always makes sense to send a follow-up email or message. Ask if he has read your earlier message and if he would still be interested in your proposal. When it comes to business proposals, it pays to be relentless with your pitches. Don't give up if you really want to rent advertising space on a website that's relevant to your dropshipping business.

- Track the performances of your ads. This is something that a lot of dropshippers often ignore and take for granted. Tracking and monitoring the results from your various ads allow you to determine which ads are working and which ads are a waste of money.

Monitoring ad performance also provides you insights on how to improve your advertisements.

- Try A/B testing for your advertisements. This is a great way to determine what types of ads work and what doesn't work. This testing method involves creating two types of ads with intentional differences e.g. two ads with the exact same message but a different headline – used to test which headline is most effective. You then run the ads for a specific period of time. During the test run, you should track the ads and gather information with regards to clicks, views, conversion rates, etc. At the end of the testing period, you compare the statistics for both types of ads.

5. Start a Newsletter

Almost everyone these days have an email address. You need an email address to sign up with anything online. You need it to sign up with Facebook. You need it to be able to upload videos on YouTube. You need it to be able to send or receive money through PayPal. You need it in order to digitally transact with government agencies. And so on and so forth. Why am I saying this? Because I want you to know of the ubiquity of email messaging and realize how huge a market it is when it comes to online promotion. I want you to realize how effective a newsletter will be in reaching out to both your established and potential customers.

But what exactly is a newsletter? In the simplest of terms, it's a content-delivery model that involves sending content to subscribers through email. I'm sure that you have come across blogs or websites wherein you are asked to subscribe by entering your email address into a form. That is a perfect example of a newsletter. Most blogs and websites these days utilize a newsletter to stay in touch with current readers as well as to recruit new subscribers. You can use the same model to grow the customer base for your dropshipping business. This is especially true if your dropshipping business revolves around an interesting niche that often gets news and media coverage. Starting a newsletter allows you to update your customers and subscribers about these latest developments.

Starting a newsletter is not that difficult. If you are a skilled programmer, you can choose to build it from scratch. If you are not a programmer, don't worry because there are tools out there that can help you create a newsletter with ease. There are companies like Aweber and MailChimp that enable you to create and build a newsletter in just a few minutes. Integrating tools and programs like Aweber into your blog and website is also hassle-free. In most cases, it is just a matter of copying and pasting code.

Here are a few tips on how you can get the most out of your newsletter:

A. Provide valuable and informative content, not just sales pitches.

Receiving sales messages over and over again can be annoying as hell. We all know that and we have all experienced that. I understand that you are running a dropshipping business and that you want to sell to the people who have subscribed to your newsletter. But everything doesn't have to be about sales and money. There should be a balance between sales pitches and informative content in your newsletter. Always keep in mind that your subscribers can easily unsubscribe with just a click of the mouse button. To make sure that they don't do such a thing, you should send them informative content every now and then.

B. Don't overdo it.

For example, sending a message every day is overdoing it. You are not running a news business wherein you need to inform people about events every single day. Only send a message through your newsletter if it's important or if it's content that you think your subscribers will find informative or helpful. Put yourself in the shoes of your subscribers and ask yourself the question: "Is this something that can help me?" If the answer is yes, click on the "Send" button. If the answer is no, don't send it. Your subscribers are probably subscribed to countless other newsletters. You will only be clogging their inboxes if you send messages too often.

C. Be direct in your messaging.

As a lot of marketers often like to say, keep it simple, stupid (KISS). The attention span of online readers are so low that if you don't grab their attention within the first few seconds, you will lose them. They will click on the delete button and move on to the next message. Online users usually don't have the time to read through blocks of text. Looking at a long email message can be too intimidating to a lot of people. In short, getting the attention of your subscribers requires brevity. Don't write a two-paragraph message if you can get your point across in just a single paragraph. Don't write two sentences if you can make your point in just one sentence.

D. Use your newsletter as the announcement platform for discounts, promos, coupons, and other sales-related offers.

This strategy provides an incentive for people to remain subscribed to your newsletter. If they unsubscribe, then they will miss out on your future promos and rewards programs. In fact, if you have high quality products, your subscribers will be looking forward to receiving updates about promos and discounts.

E. Instruct your subscribers to add your newsletter address to their contacts list.

In a lot of cases, your messages especially if you are sending them through an automated platform like Aweber will be tagged as spam or unimportant by email providers. If your messages go straight to the spam folder, then less people will read them. This is why it's important that you inform them to add your address to their contacts list. This way, your messages won't get buried in the spam folder.

F. Make it as easy as possible for people to subscribe to your newsletter.

Make the subscription form very prominent on your website or blog. It should be one of the first things that visitors see when they land on your website. The best way to do this is to create a pop-up window which appears the moment your website finishes loading on a visitor's browser. Use a direct call-to-action in telling people to subscribe to your newsletter. Furthermore, you should ask for minimal details when asking people to subscribe. Just asking for people to input their email address is enough. If you start asking about their age, or their location, etc., these can turn them off and they end up not completing the subscription process.

G. Promote your newsletter in other online platforms you are using like social media sites.

If you have a sizable following on Facebook, it would make complete sense to tell them about your newsletter. Inform them that they will be receiving important updates about your business and products on their email inboxes. If they find you interesting, they will be more than willing to subscribe to your newsletter.

6. Email Marketing

This is very similar to starting a newsletter. Sending content to your customers via a newsletter is the most common form of email marketing. It would be redundant if I discuss this matter all over again. However, there are certain points that I would like to discuss with regards to email marketing that I haven't already discussed in the newsletter section. You see, email marketing is an industry in itself and newsletter marketing falls under it. Email marketing encompasses all marketing strategies that involve email.

Email marketing is a very powerful promotional technique. The trick lies on how good you are in building your email list. As the term implies, an email list is a list of contacts that you think will be interested in buying your products. There are various ways on how to build your email list. Starting a newsletter is one of these ways. Buying email lists from other people is also a good strategy. However, you have to be careful when purchasing email lists because scams are rampant here. You should only buy email lists from reputable sources.

Another great email marketing strategy is collaboration. What you do is collaborate with another online entrepreneur. There are various types of deals that you can enter into. You can rent the other entrepreneur's email list. You can cross-promote each other's businesses. That is you promote the entrepreneur's products in your own email list. He should do the same with his email list. This is a great way to reach out to new and potential customers. Not only do you see an increase in sales, you will also see an increase in the number of people subscribing to your email list.

7. Create a Lead Page

A lead page is basically a standalone website that serves as an entry point for another website. Before anything else, the term "lead page" is a broad term. It is most commonly used to describe a website that collects email addresses and other contact information of visitors. However, that is not the definition we are going to use in the context of dropshipping. In our case, a lead page is a website that you use to drive more traffic to your main dropshipping website. This means that the lead page is a marketing tool, nothing more and nothing less. You use it to attract traffic then redirect the traffic to your main dropshipping business website.

Your main goal in creating a lead page is to convince people why they should buy your products. In other words, it's a glorified sales pitch. You follow three simple steps when developing the content for the lead page. The first step is to remind visitors of the problems or issues they are having relevant to your products. For example, if you are selling weight loss products, you are going to talk about why being overweight is bad and how it can lead to a lot of diseases.

The second step in developing the content for your lead page is to offer a solution to the problems the visitors are dealing with. In our example, you are going to offer your weight loss products as the solution. This is where you go in-depth about the merits and benefits of your products. You put everything in there. This step is crucial because this is where visitors will make the decision of whether they are going to buy your product or not. You have to be convincing with your pitch.

The third and last step in developing content for your lead page is to write the call-to-action. You reminded visitors about their weight problems, you told them about your awesome weight loss products, now it's time to tell them to buy these products. This is where you redirect people to your main website where they can order and pay for the products. Just a simple linked button that says "Buy Here Now!" will do. Since the visitor is ready to buy, you just have to redirect him or her to the sales page.

To get the most out of lead pages, you should consider creating several of them. This strategy is effective if you are selling different products in your dropshipping website. Creating one lead page for each product category is something you should consider doing. Sure, it's going to take a lot of your time but it's worth it.

8. Collaborate with Online Influencers

Have you ever come across the term "influencer marketing"? If you haven't already, allow me to define it for you. It's basically an online marketing strategy that involves paying internet influencers to promote your product. An online influencer is anyone who has a sizable following or reputation on the internet. An online influencer could be anyone. It could be a make-up artist with thousands of subscribers on YouTube. It could be a video gamer with millions of followers on Twitch. It could be a fashion enthusiast with thousands of followers on Instagram. It could be a blogger whose blog attracts millions of hits a day.

In short, influencer marketing is the online version of celebrity endorsements. You simply pay online celebrities to endorse and help promote your products. For example, let's say that you run a dropshipping business that sells a line of makeup kits. You go to YouTube and look for channels that focus on makeup tutorials. You find the most popular ones and get in touch with the owners of the channels. Send them proposals informing them that you are going to pay them if they can use your products for their next makeup tutorials. Not all of them are going to respond but there are those who will be interested. You negotiate the deal and that's it. You send the products, the influencer uses these in their videos, and you pay them for their efforts. That's basically how influencer marketing works.

Influencer marketing is a great way to build your business and brand. Sure, it will cost you money but it's completely worth it if you deal with the right team of influencers. And it's the best strategy to reach your target customers. In our example, influencers in the makeup industry command the respect and attention of thousands of people who are genuinely interested in makeup products. If you own a business that sells makeup products, dealing with these influencers provides you with a direct line to your target customers.

9. Start a Blog

I'm sure that you have heard this before. And I'm going to say it again. If you want to market products online, you need to start a blog. Don't listen to people who downplay the importance of a blog. They will tell you that it's a waste of time. Well, I'm telling you that they are completely wrong. Blogging is a very powerful strategy if you play your cards right. Since you are going to blog in connection to your dropshipping business, there are two ways you can approach it. You can either host the blog within your business website or you can create a separate website using a different domain.

Personally, I would recommend the latter option for several reasons. First of all, if you are going to host the blog within your main website, it will often be very difficult to find. It can create clutter or even confusion. The reason I want you to create the blog as a completely separate entity is that it will be easier to manage. A separate website also offers flexibility and more control over the types of content that you publish. You can install plugins, widgets, and all sorts of tools without compromising your main business website.

As far as the content of the blog is concerned, you should solely focus on creating content that's related to your business and products. It's your own way of providing additional content for your customers. For example, you have a product that is too sophisticated that customers often don't know how to use it properly. Well, you can use your blog to write in-depth tutorials or guides on how such a product is used. You can write anything on your blog but always make sure that it's relevant to your business. If you sell beauty and health products then your blog should be about beauty and health as well. That's the content that your customers need so that's the type of content you are going to provide them.

10. Collaborate With Other Dropshippers

Collaborating with other dropshippers is all about cross-promotion. You collaborate with the hope that you get to promote each other's products. Hell, you can even collaborate with your competitors. Here's what you need to do. Look for dropshippers that are in the same niche as you. They should be selling products that are relevant to your own products. Write them a proposal letter informing them if they would be interested in collaborating with you. You tell them about your products and how these could be a good fit for their existing customers. The catch is that you will also promote their products to your own customers. It's a win-win situation for both parties so most entrepreneurs will find it hard to ignore the proposal.

So basically, you promote their products and in return they promote your products. How you promote each other's products depends on your negotiations. For example, you can promote each other's products on your respective websites. You can tap into each other's email lists or newsletters. You can offer discounts through a referral system. In short, there are various collaboration tactics you can choose from.

When collaborating with other dropshippers, make sure that you always deliver your end of the bargain. This creates trust and lasting business relationships that may benefit you in the long run. In the dropshipping industry, creating and nurturing connections is very important. A former collaborator might refer you to a supplier or manufacturer who can produce your products at much cheaper costs. Or you might get tips on how to drive your production costs down so that you can increase your profit margins. These are just a few of the benefits you can get by nurturing connections with other dropshippers.

Chapter Summary

I'm not going to lie. Promoting and marketing your dropshipping business is going to take a lot of your time, money, and resources. It comes with the territory. However, I have to remind you that although these are costs, they are also investments. The time, money, and resources you spend on your dropshipping business are investments that will return to you as rewards down the road. This is the kind of mentality you should cultivate. If you treat costs as irredeemable expenses, then you are doing it wrong.

Conclusion

Before anything else, I would like to congratulate you for reading this book up to this point. That only shows that you are truly serious in pursuing opportunities that will earn you sustainable passive income. Being serious about it is a good start. It also prepares you in developing the right mindset. As I've mentioned in the beginning of this book, having the right mindset is *crucial* to your success. Most of the people who fail in this journey do so because they didn't have the right mental approach. They were lazy. They got discouraged too easily. They didn't have patience. If you truly read this book and follow it up by implementing the tips and strategies discussed within, I am confident that you are going to reach your passive income goals.

Before anything else, I would like to congratulate you for getting this far. The fact that you made it to this page means that you are truly serious in starting and building a successful dropshipping business. You have put your mind into it and you are ready to go for it. Here's the good news. If you've read and understood every chapter in this book, then you have all the knowledge you need to be successful in the dropshipping industry. That is not an exaggeration. You just have to implement everything that you've read here and you will be on your way towards success.

Of course, there is no *guarantee* that you are going to be successful. I'm lying to you if I'm going to claim that you are going to achieve success 100%. That's not what I'm telling you in this book. My main intention in writing this book was to provide you with the knowledge you need to dramatically increase your odds of achieving success in the industry. What you do with this knowledge is up to you. Think of this book as a guide, a mentor, or let's just say a reference book. It helps you get things done. It helps you nurture the right business mindset. It helps you decide on which directions to take. It helps you weigh your options. I wrote the book to guide you towards success not to hand over to you on a silver platter.

As I've said numerous times in this book, running a dropshipping business seems simple but in reality, it can be challenging. There are so many gears going on at the same time and you have to manage every single one of these gears. I'm not saying this to discourage you. I'm saying it to make sure that you know what to expect. I need you to be realistic about your goals and be practical about your plans in achieving them. Going in with the wrong assumptions and unrealistic expectations will most likely set you up to a disastrous start. Getting started the right way requires that you know what to expect and that you are aware of the risks.

Another very important point I need to remind you about is that it takes time to build a successful dropshipping business. Don't buy into the myth that dropshipping is your ticket to fast cash and instant riches. There is no such thing. You could get lucky and earn a lot early but that's very unlikely. Your best chance in becoming successful is to work harder and smarter and focus on building the business with a long-term plan. Don't fall into the trap of rushing things. Rushing doesn't fast-track you to success. In fact, it usually sets you up for failure.

Now, before you go out there and start building your dropshipping business, I have one last piece of advice to give you. DON'T GIVE UP AT THE FIRST SIGN OF FAILURE. In most cases, the difference between failed dropshippers and successful dropshippers is that the latter persevered while the former gave up at the first sign of trouble. Most dropshippers make almost zero profits on their first weeks or months. They lose money. Their websites get inundated with error after error. Their suppliers bail out on them.

There's a good chance that these will happen to you. But you shouldn't let these deter your ultimate goal of building a successful and profitable online business. Learn from these mistakes and failures and just keep moving on. There's a positive side to these mistakes and failures. They'll teach you not to make the same mistakes again. As you learn more lessons and gain tons of experience, you'll get better in running the business. It gets better and better from this point on.

That's it. If you've read the entirety of this book, you're ready to play the dropshipping game. Good luck with your journey and I can't wait to hear about your success story down the road. To success, cheers!

The End

Thank you very much for taking the time to read this book. I tried my best to cover as many ways to earn passive income as I could. If you found it useful please let me know by leaving a review on Amazon! Your support really does make a difference and I read all the reviews personally so can I understand what my readers particularly enjoyed and then feature more of that in future books.

I also pride myself on giving my readers the best information out there, being super responsive to them and providing the best customer service. If you feel I have fallen short of this standard in any way, please kindly email me at **michael@michaelezeanaka.com** so I can get a chance to make it right to you. I wish you all the best with your journey towards financial freedom!